Anstey's Party Walls

Anstey's
Party Walls

and what to do with them

Updated by Graham North

SIXTH EDITION

Published by RICS Business Services Limited
a wholly owned subsidiary of
The Royal Institution of Chartered Surveyors
under the RICS Books imprint
Surveyor Court
Westwood Business Park
Coventry CV4 8JE
UK

ISBN 1 84219 201 9

First edition 1986
Second edition 1988
Third edition 1991
Fourth edition 1996
Fifth edition 1998
Sixth edition 2005

Illustrations by Michael Cromar

The royalties from the sale of this book go to the John Anstey
Foundation, a charitable trust.

Typeset by Columns Design Ltd., Reading
Printed in Great Britain by Arrowsmith, Bristol

Contents

Contents

Introduction

A note to the reader

Why is it that some owners think that their neighbours
do not have any rights to do building work? Why do
those same owners want to obstruct an extension – when
they have already built theirs? Alas, human nature being
what it is, common sense and logic are not always at the
fingertips of those affected by construction work. This is
why the *Party Wall etc. Act* 1996 is such an effective
statute, permitting works along a boundary to a
neighbour's property, within a clear framework.
Surveyors, within this framework, can agree the manner
of such works and help to minimise their impact on the
Adjoining Owners.

It is also, of course, why this book, now in its sixth
edition, is such an effective publication. Covering all
aspects of party walls in both a practical and entertaining
manner, it aims to bring confidence to and restore the
sense of humour of those called upon to deal with the
type of neighbours mentioned above.

The original edition of *Party Walls and what to do with
them* was conceived back in the days of the *London
Building Acts (Amendment) Act* 1939 (referred to
hereafter as the LBA). The provisions of that Act have

now, of course, been extended by the 1996 Act to the whole of England and Wales. This book deals only with the 1996 Act as it applies to England and Wales, and does not pretend to be an exposition of the general law.

Indeed, this book is not an annotated Act or a clause-by-clause exposition of the Act at all – but rather a narrative. The Act is paraphrased in places, and extracts are quoted from it at times, but large chunks of it are not provided. You may sometimes need, therefore, to have a copy of the Act to hand to understand the authors' remarks.

In fact, the authors would stress that if you are to deal adequately with party wall matters as a practitioner, you will find it essential to keep the Act by you at all times. Even better, perhaps, to have an annotated version of the Act, either the Pyramus & Thisbe Club's 'The Green Book' or An Introduction to the Party Wall etc. Act 1996 (also by John Anstey, and Victor Vegoda), published by Lark Productions. As John Anstey used to point out, whenever you ask a question of a real expert, his first action will always be to reach for his copy of the Act in order to check its wording precisely.

Readers will find parts of this book very repetitious, if they read it from cover to cover. That is because the authors have tried to make each chapter as complete in itself as possible, without sending the reader backwards and forwards looking for other necessary bits of information. Nevertheless, they have cross-referenced it where they felt that extended ancillary information elsewhere in its pages might be helpful.

Much of what goes on with regard to party walls is governed by convention and common sense between surveyors, backed up by relevant case law. A lot of this book consists of the authors' personal opinions as to what is right or not, and they would have the readers believe that those bits are the most reliable. They have tried to make it clear where their advice is unsupported (and can therefore be taken as gospel), and where there is only legal authority for something, which should only be relied upon until the next leading case.

The original author (of the first five editions) of this book was John Anstey, founder and partner in Anstey Horne & Co., a leading firm of party wall surveyors. First persuaded to specialise in party walls by his father, Bryan Anstey, John went on to deal with well over 3,000 party wall cases, founded the Pyramus & Thisbe Club for party wall surveyors, served on the RICS Committee on Party Wall Procedures, helped to draft the 1996 Act, and lectured, wrote, sang and performed on the subject as often as possible.

Graham North, the new author for this sixth edition of the book, worked first as John's assistant and later alongside him as his partner. With John never afraid of voicing his views and thoughts, Graham became very familiar with his opinions over the years. He is therefore ideally placed both to continue John's line of thought in this edition, to consolidate (or, where he wishes, to argue against) his opinions, and to bring case law and other references up to date.

On the matter of updating, Graham would stress that John's original words and wisdom have by no means suffered from the passage of time. Much of what he wrote is not only relevant today, but in some cases, more true today than when he was alive. Nevertheless, Graham has agreed to take on John's mantle as expert, and make alterations and additions where the march of time has rendered these necessary. To avoid cutting between the words of the two authors, he has also agreed to merge his authorial voice with that of John's – so that the reader may read the whole book seamlessly, without worrying about who is speaking at any particular time.

John and Graham did not agree on everything. Indeed, those who knew John well will confirm that he would have been unlikely to take on a partner who was not prepared to give his own opinion, with adequate deference of course. Where Graham disagrees with John's thinking, he has made this clear in the text – giving readers two expert points of view for the price of one. Further arguments are of course welcome from readers, as for the first five editions. Many such comments sent in were included (or refuted) in earlier editions of the book.

When this book was first published, it seemed to many to represent a watershed in surveying 'textbooks', dealing with technical issues in a practical, informative, lively and humorous way. Even those with no real interest in party walls, but using the book as reference, remarked how much they enjoyed reading it. It is hoped that this new edition will continue this worthy tradition: providing an introduction for those new to the subject, expert arguments and analysis for those more experienced, and a stream of good humour to oil the wheels of all the technical information.

Readers of the book will quickly notice one tricky aspect of it, unrelated to party walls. For the sake of brevity and fluency of reading, the authors refer throughout to all manner of people in the masculine form (as 'he', 'his' and so on). As the cases noted in this book indicate, women, as well as men, can become embroiled in party wall disputes. Women naturally also solve such disputes, in the role of surveyors and as part of the legal profession. Let it be understood then, that references to the masculine include the feminine – except where this would make no sense whatsoever.

Since the 1996 Act became law in 1997, there have been a few more cases on party wall matters, the most important of which are considered in Chapter 16. However, in the main the courts are encouraging owners to settle litigation by referring matters back to the surveyors, or the Third Surveyor. This gives those surveyors the opportunity to apply their knowledge and experience fairly and independently – and can only serve to enhance the reputation of the profession along the way. It can safely be said that John would have been very pleased with such a development. It is to be hoped that the advice given in this new edition serves to continue the good work.

Graham North

John Anstey

The appointment of surveyors

The activities of surveyors are so central to party wall proceedings that it is probably helpful to deal with their appointment and their power straight away. Just before doing so, though, it may help to define some of the terms we're about to use in relation to their activities.

First of all, it's important to be clear as to what an **'owner'** is. An owner is defined in the *Party Walls etc. Act* 1996 as including:

a) 'a person in receipt of...the rents or profits of land';
b) 'a person in possession of land otherwise than as a mortgagee or as a tenant from year to year...';
c) 'a purchaser of an interest in land under a contract for purchase or under an agreement for a lease...'

A **Building Owner** is the owner who intends to do any work under the Act, exercising his rights or incurring obligations, while an **Adjoining Owner** owns or occupies 'land, buildings, storeys or rooms adjoining those of the Building Owner'. The word 'adjoining' is defined to include any property within three metres or six metres when the provisions of section 6 of the Act come into play[1]. Each and every 'owner' is entitled to his

[1] See Chapter 3.

surveyor. We will define 'surveyor' a little further on in this chapter.

If there is any dispute between owners, then it is to be 'determined in accordance with section 10' of the 1996 Act. There are always two courses open to owners, assuming that they can't agree upon the works in the first place: to agree instead upon one surveyor to sort the matter out; or each to select a surveyor. We're going to look at the first option first – partly because it is not used as often as it might be with advantage.

The 'Agreed Surveyor'

A man jointly selected is called an Agreed Surveyor; 'agreed' means, of course, agreed between the two owners (see page 6 for what exactly 'surveyor' means). The words of the relevant section of the 1996 Act are '...shall concur in the appointment of one surveyor'. Why agree on one surveyor? Well, it's simpler for one thing, to have one person working for both sides – and frequently cheaper too. And can such a surveyor really work for both sides? Yes – if he is acting properly. A good party wall surveyor operates in a judicious manner at all times, regardless of who appointed him. It is therefore part and parcel of his job to ensure that Mr Black and Mr Blue, even if they are wildly at odds with each other, *both* have their rights respected and enforced, even to the extent (fairly frequently) of telling both of them that they cannot do what they would like to do.

We go into this question of impartiality a little later on in this chapter, in more detail. For now, suffice it to say that an Agreed Surveyor must exercise even more care than one appointed on one side only. Party wall surveyors are

A good party wall surveyor

always (when acting properly!) impartial, but they should especially be seen to be so when they were originally appointed by one owner, and the other subsequently concurred in that choice. And of course, there is no-one there to check their first chosen solutions to any problem. An Agreed Surveyor should therefore look twice or more at any of his decisions before promulgating them or putting them into effect.

A Building Owner may, if a difference is anticipated, nominate his intended surveyor at the same time as serving his notice. The Adjoining Owner should be quite prepared to accept that surveyor to act between the parties, provided either that the surveyor is already known to him by repute, or that the works are small and the surveyor appears to be qualified to deal with them. John, on more than one occasion, and on behalf of one particular Building Owner, had to serve notice affecting properties which turned out to be owned by people or companies by whom he had previously been appointed in similar cases. These parties then concurred in the selection of him as surveyor. It may also happen – but usually less often – that the party on whom notice was served, while previously unknown to the surveyor in question, decides that that surveyor has a nice honest face and that it would be quite safe to leave the whole matter in his hands.

This didn't happen to John all that often – and on only one occasion did it cause any embarrassment. In that case, the original Adjoining Owner decided in turn to redevelop and appointed John as (now) the Building Owner's Surveyor. The original developer concurred in his position as Agreed Surveyor, but conflict arose when a flaw in the *earlier* award came to light as a result of the *later* work. Both parties then wanted John to side with them exclusively, which was impossible. Despite the unhappy outcome of that particular job, John did not allow the occurrence to deter him from accepting similar appointments. Neither should you – even assuming that you have an honest face.

For small works, it is an even better idea to concur in the selection of an Agreed Surveyor. One perceived flaw in party wall procedures under the Act is that the cost of producing an award in relation to the cost of the works can be disproportionate. If the owner of a small terraced house in a small provincial town wants to carry out an improvement to his property affecting both his neighbours, the cost of paying three different surveyors could be ridiculously high, even if they were all moderate in their charges. The appointment of an Agreed Surveyor reduces these costs significantly. Several people are working on a method of imposing the 'Agreed Surveyor' system on small works, and if anyone comes up with a good method, steps will be taken to try to bring it into force by legislation.

A few notes of warning on appointments are appropriate here. Later on in the progress of a dispute, power is given for one owner to make an appointment on behalf of another who has neglected to do so. However, that does not mean (*pace* some solicitors who tried it on once in a case with which John was involved) the power simply to nominate *your* surveyor as the 'agreed' one. It has also been known for some owners and/or their surveyors to invite an Adjoining Owner to accept them as agreed, which is equally unacceptable.

Sometimes a Building Owner will serve a notice, but not give the name of his surveyor if a dispute arises, or will put on the notice that his surveyor is to 'be confirmed'. The Adjoining Owner may then dissent and appoint his own surveyor, in the knowledge that he is entitled to his own surveyor. The Building Owner may then attempt to appoint that surveyor as the Agreed Surveyor. Before accepting the role of Agreed Surveyor in an instance such as this, the surveyor should check that the Adjoining Owner is happy with the arrangement. Section 10(1) allows each owner to appoint his own surveyor, and the Adjoining Owner may have thought that that was what he was getting, rather than an Agreed Surveyor.

It is sadly the case that more and more owners find it hard to believe that a surveyor can act independently. One can only hope that by the end of the procedures they will understand that party wall surveyors do just that.

Appointing individual surveyors

We must return again now to Messrs Black and Blue. They are both rich men (though they will be a lot poorer by the time they've paid their surveyors for all the differences they're about to have) and rather than an Agreed Surveyor, they propose each to appoint their own surveyor, under section 10(1)(b) of the 1996 Act. Whom can they appoint? 'Surveyor' is not, unlike 'architect', a protected term in law, and therefore they can appoint anyone. Under the *London Building Acts (Amendment) Act* 1939 (LBA), it was argued that one could appoint oneself. However, this possibility no longer exists, as a 'surveyor' is defined in section 20(1) of the 1996 Act as 'any person not being a party to the matter... '. So anyone else will do: please not an accountant or a solicitor, but mother, sister, brother, aunt, or nephew would be bearable.

Let's go a little further than 'whom can you appoint?' and ask: 'whom should you appoint?' Tempting as it is to recommend that you restrict yourself to the members of the Pyramus & Thisbe Club[1], the answer should perhaps be more general in a publication of this sort. A party wall surveyor should be well versed with the party wall procedures, because their little peculiarities, with which you are only just beginning to be acquainted, demand specialist knowledge and understanding. This, rest assured, narrows the field very considerably. It is

[1] For a description of this eminent body, see Appendix V.

desirable that your chosen man should have a technical qualification, if only to impress the opposition, and he should be accustomed to dealing with structural matters, probably as an architect, engineer or building surveyor.

Of course, this level of expertise may not be essential for a dispute over a boundary wall, but Messrs Black and Blue are beginning as we mean to go on, by assuming that appalling complications are going to arise, and that therefore only the best original choices will do. They may know someone suitable, or know someone who knows someone, or they can ask one of the professional institutions for some suggestions. Never forget, however, that the authors of this book strongly recommend concurring on an Agreed Surveyor if possible.

In the early years of the Act's operation, there appeared to be more surveyors based in London who were familiar with party wall matters than elsewhere. However, even then – and more so now, as time goes on – there could be no justification for appointing someone from the metropolis whose every visit to a provincial site was going to involve three hours travelling time, unless it was quite clear that local gentlemen were not suitably qualified. With the rapid expansion of the Pyramus & Thisbe Club to all parts of England and Wales, it is now unlikely that there is not someone within easy travelling distance of a job who is well aware of the niceties of the Act – or at least has access to colleagues who will help if he gets into difficulties. If someone other than a local man is appointed, he should not expect to charge for travelling to a distant site (and nor should a provincial gentleman charge for travelling to London), while his rates should be commensurate with the job, rather than his metropolitan expectations.

By the way, the Act says 'appoint a surveyor'. It does not say 'appoint a firm of surveyors'. You cannot therefore appoint 'Messrs Bright Sheep and Woolly', or even 'a partner in Quite Blank (and Abruptly)', although it might just be all right to nominate 'the senior partner in Jackson Fawcett and Nash', as that would be a particular individual. It is much better, however, to appoint Ms Nash by name, if that is who you want.

Impartiality

One thing must be made very clear. Once a surveyor has been appointed under the Act, whether as Agreed Surveyor or as any other kind, then he must forthwith adopt a judicial and impartial attitude to the settlement of disputes. In some cases, he may have previously been acting as the agent of his client, at the very least in the service of notices, and in some matters he may well continue to do so. However, in all matters where he is acting in his capacity as a party wall surveyor, he must be an arbitrator, not an agent. It is implicit in the whole way that section 10 is drawn that surveyors are to work together to settle matters, not in opposition to each other[1]. It is particularly difficult for an architect, who may well be expected by his client to deal with party wall matters on a small job as part of his general duties, to switch from the impassioned agent seeking the speedy and inexpensive completion of his beautiful design, to the disinterested surveyor equally ready to heed the needs of the next-door neighbour, and thus perhaps protract the

---

[1] And see *Selby v Whitbread*, Chapter 16.

job while adding to its cost. Difficult it may be, but he must do it, if he is properly to fulfil his function under the Act.

The 'Third Surveyor'

Let us suppose that Mr Black appoints Mr P McCartney as his surveyor, and Mr Blue appoints Mr N Kennedy, in an attempt to ensure that something harmonious comes out of the whole affair. What is the first thing that these two must do? It is not, as so many seem to think, to meet and agree a schedule of condition[1], or start discussing an award[2], or even, which is regrettably uppermost in some so-called professionals' minds, negotiate their fees. It is, in fact, to select a Third Surveyor. So much is this a part of the initial process, that it is made part of the same sub-section, 10(1)(b): 'each party shall appoint a surveyor and the two surveyors so appointed shall forthwith select a third surveyor'. There is very good reason for this happening so quickly. At the outset, there should be no friction between the surveyors on any point – in theory there should *never* be any friction between them, but in practice there often is – and it should be comparatively easy to choose the umpire. If they wait until there is a point needing the umpire's decision, they may not be able to agree on anything, including the umpire's name. It is therefore as well to agree a name at the outset.

The same strictures, only more so, apply to the selection of Third Surveyors as to the first two. There are many people whom you might be quite happy to meet as 'the other surveyor', but whom you would not be enthusiastic

[1] See Chapter 4.
[2] See Chapter 6.

about being called upon to sit in judgment on a knotty point. Regrettably, all too often, people who should know better put forward as potential Third Surveyors men or women whom you, as a sensible reader, would not trust to tell you the time of day. At the time of writing, there are no more than about half a dozen people whose names are regularly put forward and accepted by serious practitioners in party wall matters. You should only need a Third Surveyor in exceptionally tricky circumstances, and your selected arbiter therefore must be capable of dealing with difficult and uncommon situations. It's not a sinecure.

It is usual for the Building Owner's Surveyor to suggest three names, and for the Adjoining Owner's Surveyor to select one of them[1]. In our case, Mr McCartney might suggest Mr S Morrissey, Mr M Jagger or Mr R Dwight, and Mr Kennedy choose the last named.

What happens if the first two surveyors, even at the outset, cannot agree upon a Third Surveyor, so that even when offered such a rich choice as that put forward by Mr McCartney, Mr Kennedy is happy with none of them, and suggests instead Mr C Davis, Mr E Kleiber, or Mr L Slatkin? Mr McCartney likes none of them, and no other names that he suggests (Mr R Williams, Ms D Ross or Mr J Rotten) are any more acceptable. The writers of the Act have at least thought of this eventuality: either or both parties can apply to the 'Appointing Officer', a person so chosen by the local authority, to nominate the Third Surveyor.

---

[1] A form for this purpose, 'Selection of the Third Surveyor', is included in the RICS *Party Wall Legislation and Procedure – Notices and Letters* CD-ROM.

While the Greater London Council (GLC) existed, there was an officer known as the 'Superintending Architect', one of whose minor functions was to appoint Third Surveyors. John liked to tell of the time when he and another distinguished building surveyor (Donald Ensom) approached the GLC, offering to cast their eyes over the Superintending Architect's list of potential Third Surveyors and provide suggestions for addition, revision and excision. They were eventually sent a copy of a two-column list: at the head of the left-hand column, 'Donald Ensom'; at the head of the right, 'John Anstey'. They felt that no further comment was required.

Who, under the new Act, is the 'Appointing Officer' who must select the Third Surveyor if the first two surveyors cannot agree? He is defined in section 20 of the Act as the 'person appointed by the local authority to make such appointments'. However, if you telephone the local authority (and note that it is the local authority for the area in which the job is located, not your office), you are likely to spend half an hour explaining to someone what this is all about, and to be no further forward. In general, the head of Building Control at the authority usually gets the task of selection, so you may as well go straight to him.

An appointment by the Appointing Officer is final – he could even appoint someone already rejected by one of the parties – and the surveyor so appointed is in exactly the same position as one agreed upon by the other two. Exactly the same procedure is followed if either party refuses to agree, or fails for ten days to answer a formal request to agree upon a Third Surveyor. The phrase used, 'refuses or for ten days after a written request neglects to...', appears quite often in section 10 of the Act and is examined in more detail later in this chapter.

Don't, we would suggest, write to your chosen Third Surveyor and tell him you've selected him. Don't even ask him if you may select him. You're probably not going to need him, so you're wasting his time by writing to him now. He can't tell at this juncture whether he will be available to act when and if you have a dispute. He might be free now, but just starting a High Court case or a holiday at the time your disagreement reaches a head. So wait till he's actually needed before popping the question. It may well be a politeness to ask a chap if he minds, in general, your putting his name forward as Third Surveyor, but if you're going to do so, do it via a brief phone call.

John held out a special offer for anyone who bought this book: they had his permission to put his name forward. Anyone who borrowed the book, however, or was reading it in the library, had to ask by phone. Graham would like to extend the special offer on his own behalf.

If the Third Surveyor dies, becomes incapable, refuses, or neglects to act, then you go back to square one and start trying to select another man acceptable to both the first two. Perhaps Mr McCartney and Mr Kennedy will jointly agree on Mr Dwight this time, but if not, then re-read the relevant pages for procedure as before.

How to appoint

How are the various surveyors appointed? The rule is: in writing. Section 10(2) of the Act states that all appointments and selections shall be in writing, to ensure that the surveyors' appointments are clearly confirmed by their owners. When selecting a Third Surveyor with the other surveyor, you may agree a name on the telephone, but you should then confirm it with the other party *in writing*, ensuring that your opposite number also acknowledges the selection.

It is common for this to be overlooked. Not only does the failure to write to each other confirming the name of the Third Surveyor mean that you are not following the Act, but it can create difficulties later. Graham has known surveyors for Adjoining Owners deny that they have ever concurred in his appointment as Third Surveyor – and without the selection having been put in writing, he has been unable to deal with the matter. (Note that if there is a published award that confirms the name of the Third Surveyor, then this is 'in writing', as both surveyors have signed it.)

Removal of surveyors

There are various provisions for ensuring that the surveyors get on with their work, or for replacing them if they cease to act, to which we shall come in due course, but there is one eventuality which is conspicuous by its absence. There is no power given to a dissatisfied owner to discharge his surveyor. Under the LBA this was implicit, but section 10(2) of the new Act makes it explicit. This is important for two reasons: firstly, it emphasises yet again the necessity for impartiality in the surveyor; and secondly, it makes it impossible for a deliberately obstructive owner to frustrate the purposes of the Act by constantly hiring and firing surveyors, thus regularly causing proceedings to start *de novo*.

The only ways in which a surveyor can cease to be the appointed surveyor are: if the job comes to an end (not stated in the Act but, *pace Marchant v Capital and Counties*[1], surely obviously so when any making good has been completed); if he dies (and even most of those Appointing Owners who desire nothing so much as to get rid of surveyors who refuse to do what they are told don't go so far as to promote that end); or if he becomes incapable of acting. Both the latter eventualities are provided for by section 10(5).

'Incapable of acting' will bear a little examination. One of John's staff once gave notice, under the Party Wall Surveyors Act 1975[2], that he intended to leave his office by more than six metres, and therefore called upon John to appoint another surveyor in his stead. John replied that as the member of staff had always been incapable of acting, he couldn't see how his departure would change things. So to clear up any confusion, what exactly does the Act mean? Would a chap who went off for four weeks' holiday be incapable, or merely neglectful? It is, in fact a critical difference, as if he is incapable, the owner who appointed him can appoint another in his place, but if he is neglectful, then the other surveyor can proceed ex parte. This will have to be considered below, but meanwhile we must concentrate on 'incapable'.

This is another instance where something which was implicit in the LBA has become explicit in the present Act. Whereas it used to be believed to be in order for a surveyor to inform his Appointing Owner that he was incapable of acting, no-one was sure if his statement to that effect was legally adequate. Section 10(5) now

---

[1] See Chapter 16.
[2] A joke.

specifically allows for the surveyor to deem himself incapable. Very rarely is his incapability a physical or a mental inability to cope. Far more often it is a diplomatic sickness of some kind. As explained above, an appointment is specific to one person: you cannot appoint a firm. Sometimes the named surveyor changes firms in the middle of a job, and what happens then depends upon the terms on which this transfer takes place. Strictly speaking, a firm could probably not stop him retaining the party wall appointment, and sometimes they have no wish to do so, so that the appointment moves with him to his new place of employment. In a firm where an experienced assistant may understand the ins and outs of a job far more than the named surveyor, it is not unknown for the surveyor to declare himself incapable of acting in order to allow the assistant to take the job with him to his new firm. At other times, either because the firm he leaves is in a position to exert strong pressure on him in other respects, or because it would not in fact be convenient for him to retain the appointment, a surveyor notifies his Appointing Owner that he is no longer capable of acting in the matter.

In such cases, the outgoing surveyor usually suggests that the bereaved owner may care to appoint (for example) Mr S Rattle, the man most suitable in the original firm to take over the work. However, there is no obligation upon the owner to do so.

Sometimes the owner will not wish to appoint anyone else from the same firm. This is particularly likely to be true if the incapability is the result of another kind of diplomatic action. As stated above, the disgruntled owner cannot sack his surveyor and, if his nerves are as strong as his sense of justice, a surveyor can go on acting even for an owner who detests and distrusts him. Very often, though, he may feel that the best way out for both parties is for him to become incapable of acting, and thus allow the owner another choice. In the authors' experience, this kind of conflict usually arises when the owner wilfully refuses to understand the Act and the surveyor's position under it, and in that case his second choice, if the latter is himself a proper party wall surveyor, is likely to prove just as unsatisfactory as the first, as he, too, will refuse to 'do what the client tells him', such as acting improperly in trying to obstruct the other owner's rights.

However the vacancy arises, whether by death or incapability – diplomatic or otherwise – under section 10(5) the 'surveyorless' owner can appoint anyone he likes to fill the gap, and the new man will 'have the same power and authority' as his predecessor. Possibly, despite the Act's silence on the point, the owner could even at this stage change his mind and concur in the selection of the remaining surveyor, but the authors have never known this to happen.

Note that if an 'Agreed Surveyor' fails to get on with things, or becomes incapable (or dies), the whole proceedings start *de novo*, so that the Adjoining Owner is not bound to concur in the Building Owner's new suggestion. If he was happy with the first man, but is not happy with the second, he can put forward his own surveyor under 10(1)(b), just as he had the power to do in the original situation.

The other matter on which the Act is silent and which is relevant at this point is: how bound is the successor by his predecessor's actions? This question arises in a similar form, and will have to be considered later[1], when dealing with changes in ownership of properties which are already involved in party wall proceedings. John's views on this matter were that any late arrival must be bound by concluded events, but free to go his own way on matters which were not yet settled. He might wish to agree upon a different Third Surveyor, but unless the other surveyor agreed to a change, an existing decision would stand. However, John retained an element of doubt on this issue – although he was far more secure in his opinion that the newcomer would be bound by an agreed schedule of condition, and was certain that he would have to accept a signed award, as well as believing that he would have the right to change an award that was still in draft.

Owner's failure to act

Suppose that the Adjoining Owner won't do anything: what then? It almost always is the Adjoining Owner who neglects to act, of course, although very occasionally you may find a Building Owner pressing on with work and refusing to appoint a surveyor. In most cases, a Building Owner who won't appoint a surveyor won't have served a notice either, although John did once receive a belated and ill-scrawled notice on which the illegible Building Owner had written 'n/a' (presumably meaning 'not applicable') where he should have inserted the name of his surveyor. Most Adjoining Owners would seek an injunction as a remedy in that case, but if a notice had been served, they could opt to appoint a surveyor on behalf of the Building Owner, who could then make an award binding the Building Owner to be a good boy for

---

[1] See Chapter 11.

the rest of the works. This, however, is unlikely, and the speculation is forcing us to get ahead of ourselves. *Revenons à nos moutons.*

If either party refuses to appoint a surveyor or, you won't be surprised to hear, neglects to do so for ten days after a written request, the other party has the power to make the appointment for him. The usual pattern is that the Building Owner serves a notice[1]; the Adjoining Owner is silent; 14 days later the Building Owner requests the Adjoining Owner to appoint a surveyor, as a dispute is deemed to have arisen; Brer Rabbit, he still lies low and says nothing; so the Building Owner now chooses a surveyor for him.

When choosing a surveyor for someone else you should use the same care as if you were choosing him for yourself. While it may never yet have happened (to the authors' knowledge) for an award to be set aside because one owner chose a bad egg as the other owner's surveyor, it remains a possibility. So choose well. Of course, it's perfectly proper to choose someone who is already involved in the job, either acting for another interest in the same building, or for another building adjoining the development. Such an action would almost certainly be cheaper, with travelling time saved, and with no need to argue the same problems with several different surveyors. And there's nothing improper in finding the cheaper option. If no suitable candidate is already in the vicinity, then use the criteria set out above and choose a man for the particular job. It is not permitted, as noted at the beginning of this chapter, to appoint your own surveyor as the 'Agreed' one. It must be someone separate.

[1] See Chapter 5.

Remember that your selection on behalf of the Adjoining Owner is no more your creature than he would be if he were your own appointment as your surveyor. John was once appointed thus, and the Building Owner said, 'Right: we can get on with it now, can't we?' John disillusioned him and proceeded to deal critically with his proposals, insisting on several changes for the benefit of 'his' owner. Sadly, but not surprisingly in this wicked world, he got no more work from that source for several years.

Surveyor's failure to act

We have probably now covered every eventuality except one, arising out of the appointment of surveyors (and you may never before have realised how much could be said on the subject). The one remaining possibility has already been alluded to briefly, and it arises when an appointed surveyor fails or refuses to act. In that case (section 10(6)), the other surveyor may proceed *ex parte*: that is to say, he may draft his own award and issue it, with all the force as if it had been agreed by the two surveyors. Again, though, the proper disinterest must be shown. The award must not confer all rights on one owner while neglecting those of the other. It must be one which you would probably have agreed with the other chap, if only he could have been bothered to do so.

It has been known for surveyors to listen too much to their Appointing Owners, and deliberately to put off signing an award because 'they were told to'. In such cases, it can have a salutary effect on them – and their owners – to issue an *ex parte* award. Apart from anything else, they can see their fees disappearing, and that often talks to such time-servers. They almost always

then rush back into action, usually challenging the
validity of the *ex parte* award. If this happens to you, you
could then refuse to withdraw the award – which of
course you wouldn't have made if it hadn't been justified
and in order – but you might agree to succeed it, not
supplant it, by a bi-partisan award. In such instances, the
second award rarely differs from the first by more than a
few words of little consequence.

Now we have one or two (and if two, three) surveyors,
and we know how to appoint them, replace them, and
that we can't displace them. What have we got them for?
Read on.

What is a party wall?

You will be relieved to know that it is very easy to tell you what a party wall is – as long as we make it clear that we're only dealing with the 1996 Act. It is either a wall standing on the land of two owners, or else however much of a wall separates the buildings of two owners. That's fairly simple, but to clarify even further, see the standard illustrations below.

The first thing to note is that the wall doesn't have to be equally astride the boundary. There's a chance that the courts might decide that half an inch in a three-foot-thick

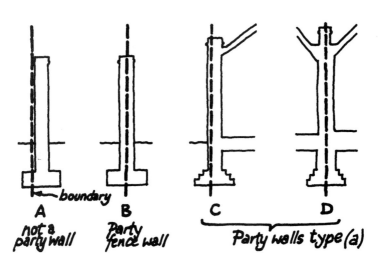

wall was a tiny mistake in what was obviously intended to be a wall wholly on the land of one owner.

The second thing to note is that this is an over-simplification of the definition of a party wall in section 20 of the 1996 Act, which makes it clear that the 'astrideness' does not include 'the projection of any artificially formed support on which the wall rests...'. The authors have always taken that to refer to foundations, howsoever formed, whether of stepped brick footings or concrete – not, however, reinforced concrete[1] – but the argument has also been advanced that this includes piers. However, apart from the fact that walls cannot really be said to rest on piers, it is noteworthy that section 2(2)(g), of which more – not much more – later, does not specifically mention piers as something which may be cut off in order to allow the raising of another wall, and sub-section (h) also refers to 'parts of any wall or building...overhanging' the next-door land, which also doesn't sound much like what a pier does. The authors' inclination is to believe that piers, provided that is all they are, and that they do not form a substantial part of the wall, should be excluded from the determination of the boundary and included within those things which may be cut off.

Nomenclature is a tricky business when dealing with party walls.

Turn now to the diagrams opposite.

The subtle difference, which you will immediately spot, between those below and those diagrams at the beginning

[1] See Chapter 3.

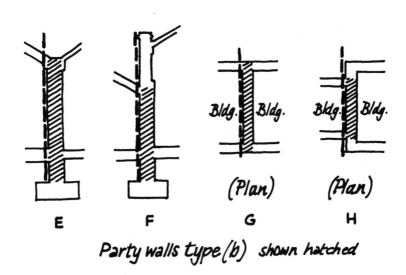

E   F   G   H

Party walls type (b) shown hatched

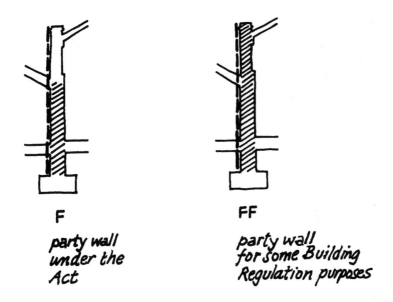

F

party wall
under the
Act

FF

party wall
for some Building
Regulation purposes

of the chapter, is that if a party wall is type (a), standing astride the boundary, then all the wall above it is a party wall, whereas if it stands wholly on the land of one owner, type (b), it ceases to be a party wall where next-door no longer encloses on it. Sideways extensions have the same status, or lack of it. Remember that in this sub-section, (b), we're only dealing with walls which stand wholly on the land of one owner, but which happen also to form, wholly or partly, an enclosure for a neighbouring building. A wall standing wholly on one owner's land, acting as a garden wall only, which has been used as an enclosing wall for a building by an Adjoining Owner, does not fall within either definition: it is therefore not a party wall (although what it is instead is open to debate).

The question has been asked: for how long does a wall have to be enclosed on before it becomes a party wall type (b)? Can a chap sneak up behind your wall when

you're not looking, slap his lean-to up against your wall, and proudly proclaim that you now can't do anything to it without his say-so? While there is as yet no legal authority on the point, learned counsel in a talk to the Pyramus & Thisbe Club[1] expressed the opinion that you would have the normal limitation period of six years in which to call upon the propped-up character to abate his trespass. Others have put forward the suggestion that as soon as he makes his enclosure he is safe, but the authors of this work find that a ridiculous proposition. There may be more merit in the argument that you need to acquire an adverse possessory (or squatter's) title over 12 years.

Following the passage of the *Land Registration Act* 2002, an owner who has enclosed upon his neighbour's wall and wishes to claim adverse possession will now have to follow the procedures of this Act. This will entail notifying the owner of the wall of your intention to claim ownership to it. No longer will an owner be able to lay claim to land or property simply by 'possession' or 'occupation', if the 12-year period expired after the 2002 Act came into force. However, an owner can still claim under the old procedures if the 12 years of 'possession' were completed prior to this Act.

It may even be argued that you can never attain party wallhood, as to butt your building against someone else's wall is a trespass: a continuing trespass as long as it's there, so that there is a continuing right of action so long as it remains there. However, as a right of support can be acquired by prescription, after 20 years you can at least rely on not being allowed to fall down.

[1] See Appendix V.

Probably a safe rule for those acquiring rights is not to think you're safe until 12 or 20 years have elapsed, and for those enclosed against to fear the worst after six.

Another word about adverse possession is relevant here. The case of *The Prudential v Waterloo*[1] shows that in certain, very particular, circumstances, it is possible adversely to possess the far side of a party wall. Be very careful therefore of former party walls revealed by demolition (or even war damage) which might fall solely into the hands of the owner of the occupied site.

There are other definitions, too, some of which lack absolute certainty, but one of which at least is crystal clear. A 'party fence wall' complies with definition (a), but has no buildings attached to it, on either side. It is therefore most commonly found in what we might call 'garden walls', standing half on each of two gardens, front or back.

Also of general application is the term 'party structure'. This is so general that it includes party walls (and, though it is not specifically stated, probably party fence walls) and also 'a floor partition or other structure separating buildings or parts of buildings approached solely by separate staircases or separate entrances'. The words 'from without' used to appear at the end of this definition in the LBA, which led to ambiguity, or at any rate to anomaly. What was the structure between the different floors of a block of flats? The flats are served by a common stair, although their front doors, on to corridors, might be argued to be 'from without'. But take a converted mansion in which the semi-basement (or

[1] See *The Great Wall of Knightsbridge*, Chapter 16.

garden flat, as it will probably be called in the sale particulars) has been severed from the ground floor, had its staircase removed, and been provided with its own front door to the outside world. Now the ceiling/floor (depending upon which way you're looking) is party, though it is unlikely to differ in construction or impact upon the parties from the structure separating the ground and first floors which, following the argument adduced above, would not be party.

For that reason, it was thought desirable in the new Act to include all such horizontal separating structures. Note that the Act does not attempt to define ownership of such divisions, and solicitors can continue happily to debate whether title extends to the joists or the floor coverings.

The term 'boundary wall' appears from time to time in the Act, but is not defined except by exclusion. At section 1(1) remarks are made about 'a boundary wall (not being a party fence wall or the external wall of a building)' and by extrapolation it would appear that a boundary wall is a fence wall standing wholly on the land of one owner. Similarly, 'the external wall of a building' appears to be one standing wholly on the land of the owner of the building attached to it. If there is open space the other side of the wall, then there are no party wall incidents, but of course if there is some other building attached to all or part of it, then it falls into type (b) (see diagram overleaf).

You should note, by the way, that because a type (b) wall is only 'party' where the two buildings are separated, many of the rights granted under section 2 do not apply. The person on whose land the wall does not stand cannot, for example, raise it. Furthermore, it probably

27

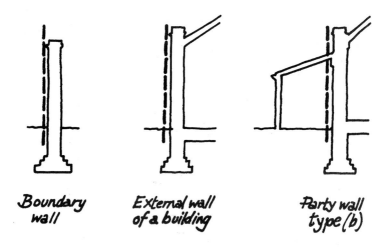

Boundary wall   External wall of a building   Party wall type (b)

stops being party if the non-owner demolishes his building which has been constructed against it without immediately rebuilding.

What do you call a wall which stands on the land of two owners, but serves only one building, as in Fig (c) on page 21? This is the kind of wall which figured in *Gyle-Thomson v Walstreet*[1] and is illustrated again on the facing page as a 'whatcha call it?' 'A party wall' is a perfectly correct answer, as it stands on the land of two owners, but it doesn't clearly enough discriminate from the more usual kind, as in Fig (d) on page 21 and from 'the external wall of a building', which it most certainly is in common parlance. A term of art for this sort of wall might be useful, but sadly, despite all of John's past efforts and those of many other illustrious party wall surveyors, no such terms have so far been invented for these curiosities.

[1] See Chapter 16.

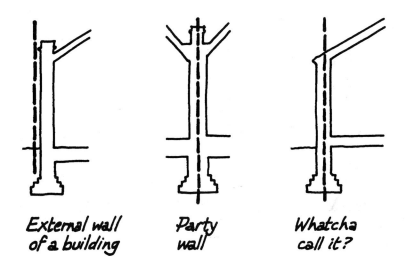

External wall
of a building

Party
wall

Whatcha
call it?

Rights of owners – and duties!

It is time to turn our attention now to owners. There are some difficult ones about, so it's vital that you (and they) are aware of what they are, and are not, allowed to do.

Graham remembers the time when a telephone call from a concerned Adjoining Owner informed him that the builders had arrived next door and seemed to be carrying out their works with a little more enthusiasm than was good for them. When told that notices had not been received or a schedule of condition taken, Graham enquired exactly what was causing the caller to worry. He was told that not only were the men over her roof and in her garden, but they were actually walking around in her loft space!

A prompt site visit by Graham in the company of the Building Owner showed that the Building Owner was carrying out works in breach of the Act. Fortunately, the Building Owner saw the error of his ways and immediately appointed a surveyor, who concluded an award with Graham so that the works could proceed (after a very short delay) in such a way as to provide adequate protection to both the Building Owner and – more importantly – the Adjoining Owner.

This is a more common occurrence than you might think. A swift response and a proactive approach from surveyors and their owners will normally bring the matter to a satisfactory resolution – but not always.

This chapter considers the rights and duties of owners, good and bad. We start off with a look at section 2 of the Act, which essentially covers works owners may wish to carry out to their party walls, then discuss excavation works under section 6 of the Act, and finally address section 1 of the Act and the question of building on the boundary.

Section 2

The first thing to note is that one tends to speak of section 2 as conferring certain rights. However, some of those rights would be there without the Act, and those items thus actually become restrictions on the owner, as he cannot do those things without notice, any more than he can do the things for which he specifically needs the power of the Act.

The second thing to note is the subtle difference between 2(2)(b) and 2(2)(e). Much of the wording is similar, but clause (b) is concerned with works which are 'necessary on account of defect or want of repair'. This may make a crucial difference to who pays for the works, so be careful, when serving notice, which clause you cite, and take care when you *receive* a notice to observe which one has been used.

Clause (a) of section 2 permits underpinning, thickening or raising a party structure; clause (b) allows demolition of a defective one; and clause (e) deals with rebuilding

31

stronger or higher simply because the Building Owner needs it. In the case of actions under most of the clauses of section 2(2), there is a specific requirement that any damage to next door should be made good. Raising has been held to include going downwards, to form a basement. In addition, any chimney stacks or flues against the wall must be raised sufficiently to keep them drawing.

As remarked above, the works in these clauses include 'thickening', which is something you would normally expect to be able to do without reference to the chap next door (and which, when it is done, is probably so done). Technically, however, you are required to serve notice that you intend to do so. Even 'making good' and 'repairing' need notice, though perhaps more in order to safeguard the apportionment of payment than for any other reason. And do you need to serve notice under the Act if you are intending merely to repoint your side of a party wall? The strict legal answer is probably yes, but you should be able to obtain your neighbour's consent to the work by friendly discussion.

For those neighbours who get on, and oh, what a refreshing change to come across such people, consent to allow each other to do certain things should not be discouraged. Indeed, surveyors should look to facilitate such co-operation.

The extent of the right given by clause (e) is really quite staggering. The Adjoining Owner can be sitting on his side of the party wall, quietly drinking his tea, writing his memoirs, fiddling his tax return, or whatever takes his fancy, when suddenly there flops on to his doormat a letter telling him that in two months all these clandestine activities (the tea drinking, for example) are going to be revealed to the world, because the man next door, who has suddenly been elevated to the status of a Building Owner, has decided that the wall between them is of insufficient strength or height for the purposes of his 'intended building'. Our innocent can, of course, usually have some screens installed at the Building Owner's expense before the demolition commences, and 'all damage occasioned by the work to the adjoining premises or to their internal finishings and decorations' will have to be made good out of the same pocket: but the disruption, the upheaval, not once but twice (when the screens go in and when they come out again) is likely to try him sorely – and although there is provision in the Act for soothing that hurt, at section 11(6)[1], it is unlikely fully to make up for everything.

There is one dramatic change in this section, compared with the LBA. Certain surveyors were of the opinion that if one side had paid for the erection of a high wall, astride their boundary, which the other side only used as a garden wall, then the Building Owner was entitled to take down the wall and rebuild it to a lesser height, provided that it still served the needs of the Adjoining Owner. This led to the case of *Gyle-Thompson v Walstreet*,[2] where the judge held that he couldn't. As this seemed patently unfair, the present Act has specifically incorporated such a right under (m). Clause (f) is another one which gives an owner a right which he may have been under the impression he already had: 'to cut into a party structure'. It doesn't say what this cutting in may be for. Usually when notice is served, it is a matter of bonding in a new partition wall, or providing the bearing

---

[1] See Chapter 10.
[2] See Chapter 16.

for a beam, but the installation of a wall safe and,
specifically, the provision of a damp-proof course are also
covered. Decorations have to be made good (again), as
they do in clause (g), which really does give the Building
Owner a right which he otherwise wouldn't have, and (h)
takes it even further. He can cut off almost anything
which projects on or over his land, whether it's a footing,
a flue, or a leaning wall, if it gets in the way of his
erecting a vertical wall against the existing structure
(although one learned authority doubts whether one can
be altogether ruthless with a leaning wall). He can also
(under the new Act) similarly cut off anything
overhanging the party wall which inhibits its raising.

Would that there were more clauses like (k), which
confers a right to do 'any other necessary works' – but
unfortunately limits itself to 'the connection of a party
structure with the premises adjoining it'. It's not quite
clear what this is meant to cover, but it is usually taken to
mean things like bonding in new cross walls or front and
rear walls to the party wall. However, it has recently
come to be very useful for the times when an old party
wall has to be left up to protect a building which is not
itself properly tied into it, because the party wall
originally formed part of the building which is now being
demolished, while the later building (now to remain) was
merely butted up against it, and perhaps block-bonded at
front and rear. Despite clause (e)[1], it is often preferable
not to take full advantage of this right, and to leave the
old party wall in place, while building an independent
wall for the new building. But then the problem arises:
how is one to hold the old wall in place until the new
wall gets up? Answer: clause (k), and fix the wall back to

[1] See above.

the continuing structure with tie rods, bolts, brackets, or whatever is necessary.

The following (true) example gives some idea of the difficulties that can arise in this area. Reliable engineering advice had been given that the only safe way of underpinning a party wall was to underpin the rear wall of the Adjoining Owner's building. If the Adjoining Owner wasn't prepared to do this, could the Building Owner do it under clause (k), and perhaps recover the costs from the Adjoining Owner? If he couldn't, would he then be responsible for any damage to the Adjoining Owner's premises, following *Brace v SE Regional Housing Association*[1]? The Third Surveyor gave his opinion that he couldn't use (k), but that it would be unjust for him to be liable.

Clause (l) allows you to change the party fence wall into a party wall, with or without rebuilding, or to raise a party fence wall, or, very exceptionally, to knock it down, even if it is in perfect repair, and rebuild it again just, it would appear, to satisfy a whim.

Clause (m) spells out in detail the right to reduce a party wall in height. The Building Owner can do so to a minimum height of two metres (ample for a garden wall for next door) or to the height currently enclosed on by the Adjoining Owner. This will be taken to include any necessary parapet, by sub-section (7).

Finally, clause (n) allows the exposure of a party wall to the elements (by demolishing one's building which used it for enclosure) only if adequate weathering is provided.

[1] See Chapter 16.

Adequacy will depend on the wall, the exposure and the time for which it is likely to endure.

Actually, it isn't finally, because we have omitted clauses (c) and (d) and haven't yet reached sub-section (3), but this detailed exposition can be so wearying that it seemed wise to put in a false summit where you could rest for a bit. The reason for omitting (c) and (d) so far, is that even extremely experienced party wall surveyors may well never have had to use either of them. Indeed, John was never sure how consistent these clauses were with sub-section (8) anyway. Clauses (c) and (d) are all about altering structures which don't comply with the statutory requirements, while sub-section (8) says that anything built before the Act shall be deemed to comply, providing it complied with whatever was in force when it was built. If so, why should anyone want to waste money on making something comply with the newer enactments? All that can be said perhaps, is that if someone feels the urge to demolish timber 'party walls', or raise fallen arches, then they can do so by following the usual procedures. However, under the new legislation, the local authority might instead instruct the Building Owner to do the work, and the latter would then have to serve notice under one or more of these sub-sections.

Sub-sections (3) to (6) deal with the responsibility for making good, arising out of the exercise of the various options above.

It is perhaps worth mentioning here, though you won't reach it in the Act until section 7(4), that you cannot place reinforced concrete on next-door's land without written consent, and that that consent must come from the Adjoining Owner, not his surveyor.

Section 6

Section 6 is curious in its differences from section 2: you can pull down a wall which reveals next door in all its nakedness without producing any plans of your proposals – or at any rate you can serve notice of your intention to do so: the surveyors will soon enough insist on the plans – but you cannot serve notice of your intention to build an independent building whose foundations may impinge upon an Adjoining Owner without accompanying it with a plan of your site and a section showing the depth to which you intend to excavate. Strange, isn't it? Many people seem to think you have a duty to show the depth of next-door's foundations, but the Act doesn't say so.

Section 6(6) states that a Foundation notice should be accompanied by plans and sections showing:

- the site and depth of any excavation the Building Owner proposes to make; and

- if the Building Owner proposes to erect a building or structure, its site.

Although it is not a requirement to show the location of the Adjoining Owner's property in relation to the site, it is a very good idea to do so. Sometimes drawings are confusing for the professional person, let alone the lay one, and if an Adjoining Owner is not sure about what is going to happen to his building, it makes him even more anxious. One amendment to the Act (which might still happen) is likely to be a requirement to include a site plan showing both the Adjoining Owner's and the Building Owner's properties.

The standard pictures to illustrate the Three Metre and Six Metre provisions (which used to be the Ten Foot and Twenty Foot provisions) appear opposite.

In the old LBA, the word 'independent' appeared in different places in the paragraphs that are now sub-sections (1) and (2) of section 6. This made the provisions hard to understand, and sometimes pointlessly negated the whole purpose of the section. The word has therefore been removed from the new Act. Furthermore, it seemed to those drafting the new provisions that it was illogical for a nearby property not to be served with notice simply because a narrow strip of someone else's land intervened. This was often the case in the City of London, where Twenty Foot (old style) notices were not legally necessary across alleys belonging to the City Corporation rather than the frontagers. Section 6(4) therefore now states that anyone within the distances specified qualifies for notice, regardless of how many ownerships there may be between. A series of five-metre shop frontages would consequently involve notice, if the six metre provisions applied, to both next door and next-door-but-one.

Only occasionally does the precise measurement of the six metres cause a problem, but you must be sure where the 45° angle is drawn from, and it is as shown: where the downward projected face of the Adjoining Owner's wall meets the bottom of his foundations. If any part of the proposed building, which can include foundations, retaining walls, and may even include drains, cuts that 45° line, then notice is necessary. While we're on precision, note also where the three metres is measured: not from wall to wall, but from nearest bit of foundation to ditto. In both cases the distance is to be measured

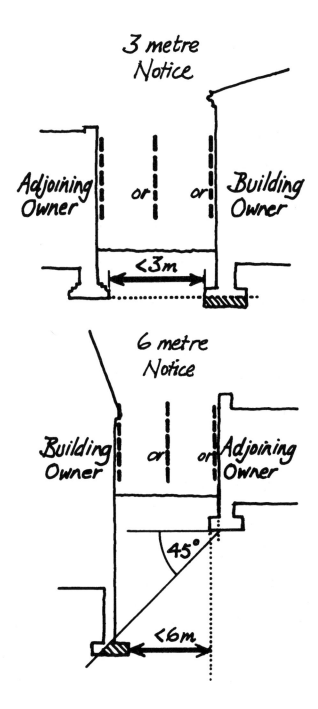

3 metre
Notice

Adjoining
Owner

or   or

Building
Owner

<3m

6 metre
Notice

Building
Owner

or   or

Adjoining
Owner

45°

<6m

horizontally, which was believed to be the case under the LBA, though not explicitly stated. In this Act it is.

By the way, the three metres or six metres can be measured in any horizontal direction, not necessarily at right angles to the boundary.

This section of course entirely serves to restrict a Building Owner, rather than to confer a right. Formerly, the Building Owner could do either of these kinds of work without so much as a by your leave. Now, he not only has to give notice, he also has to say in advance what he intends to do about 'safeguarding' the Adjoining Owner's foundations. In the authors' opinion, by far the best safeguarding of an Adjoining Owner's foundations is to leave them alone. It is preferable to design foundations so that no load is imposed on the neighbours' building or on the ground nearby. It is also generally preferable to retain the soil in the vicinity of the adjoining property by shoring or strutting, rather than exposing the foundations and underpinning them. If a building is underpinned, there is almost inevitably some movement, albeit small, but if it can be adequately retained, there may be none. There will doubtless be discussion between the surveyors on the best method in any particular case, to be settled in the usual way.

Much discussion has taken place around the country since the 1996 Act came into force about a problem which never seemed to cause any difficulties in London: do public utilities have to serve notice for excavation of trenches? There has been a subtle change in the wording of course, so that excavation alone, not construction, requires notice, but the answer seems to be that the utilities are not Building Owners within the Act. If the local authority does happen to own the road, it could be construed as the owner, but again in the opinion of the authors, it should not be necessary for it to serve notice. The costs would be wildly disproportionate, and the authority must be liable anyway for any damage that it might cause.

Section 1

Although this section, as the more numerate among you will have observed, comes before sections 2 and 6, it is far less frequently met with, and has therefore been relegated to the Third Division. Here we meet the 'boundary wall', which is not defined, but which may be deduced to be a wall standing wholly on the land of one owner and not forming part of a building – a sort of unparty fence wall. If that is all that is standing on the line of junction of the lands of two owners, a Building Owner can suggest, by notice, building a party wall or party fence wall astride the boundary. If the Adjoining Owner doesn't like the idea, then the Building Owner has to place it on his own land, but he has an absolute right to put foundations (as long as they're not reinforced) on next-door's land, with due notice. This does not, however, authorise a Building Owner to knock down an Adjoining Owner's boundary wall to replace it with a party fence wall or a party wall, and so the prior existence of a boundary wall or the external wall of a building on the Adjoining Owner's land would seem to pre-empt the possible construction of a party wall.

As far as Section 1 – Line of Junction notices are concerned, it is worth noting that there is no automatic dissent to a notice after 14 days, unlike notices served for section 2 or section 6 works. If a notice is issued by an owner to build on his own land, then as long as his notice contains the requisite information, he is free to proceed after one month, unless an Adjoining Owner dissents.

The nationwide extension of the 1996 Act puts an end to the possibility of the recurrence of an entertaining saga related by a member of the Pyramus & Thisbe Club – except, of course, on the Scottish border. A certain Building Owner served notice of his intention to build a wall on his own land with foundations protruding on to next-door's garden. He received an indignant reply telling him that he couldn't. He responded by pointing out his rights under the Act. The reply asked what that had to do with it. 'We live in the area of the Act,' said the Building Owner, 'and so you're bound to let me do it.' 'You may,' retorted the adjoining owner[1], 'but I don't.' Result, foundations on the Building Owner's land only. Obviously, the right cannot run beyond the actual boundary of the Act's operations, which in this case was the junction of the two gardens.

Finally, bear in mind that section 1 carries with it many other sections of the Act, including rights of access under section 8 and the possibility of awards under section 10.

---

[1] Note that he doesn't get capital letters, because he's outside the Act.

How to have a party wall affair

When the first edition of this book was being written, an eminent surveyor remarked to John, 'Whatever you do, explain the practical way things are done'. This chapter, with much attendant risk of repeating whole chunks of other chapters, will therefore be an attempt to describe, practically, the progress of a typical party wall job.

All too typically will come a telephone call from a client – and a client he is at this stage – telling you that he's starting work tomorrow and asking you to deal with the party walls. The first thing you must do is to stop him, and then you can start sorting him out. Find out, if necessary by having a meeting with him and his architect – perhaps his engineer too – exactly what he proposes to do; extract, invariably with difficulty, details of the proposed foundations; decide which sections of the Act are relevant; tell the client (he still is) how long he must wait while notices are served; get a letter of authority from him allowing you to serve notices on his behalf, which you may well be asked by the Adjoining Owner's Surveyor to produce as evidence of that authority; get the necessary drawings from the architect and engineer; find out who all the Adjoining Owners are; serve notice on them all, accompanied by a letter on the lines of RICS draft letter 1 from the *Party Wall Legislation and*

Procedure guidance note; and then sit back and wait. You're actually waiting for two things: the anguished cries of 'Can't I start yet?' from your (still) client; and the responses from the Adjoining Owners. As soon as you get those (ignore the anguished cries) and assuming that they don't consent to the works, a dispute has arisen and you become – proud moment – a party wall surveyor. At this point, so far as matters connected with the party wall are concerned, you no longer have a client: your erstwhile client is now your Appointing Owner.

Let us assume that we are carrying out works under section 2. After a fortnight, probably half the Adjoining Owners will have replied, but the others have now dissented by their silence. Three-quarters of the half who have replied will have named their surveyor. What is the minimum number of Adjoining Owners in this example?[1] To the remaining quarter you write politely pointing out that they must appoint someone, but to the other half you write more in the form of RICS draft letter 2 from the guidance note, which reminds them that they've had a notice, and tells them what they should be doing about it.

After a bit more of this sort of stuff, you should end up with a clutch of Adjoining Owners' Surveyors (if that is the correct collective noun). The first thing you must do is to agree upon a Third Surveyor. It's probably a good idea to try to have the same Third Surveyor for the whole site, but it's also quite likely that each Adjoining Owner's Surveyor will have his own pet likes and dislikes among the ranks of suitable candidates. Anyway, get him or them selected, and then you can get down to the affair proper.

---

[1] Eight. A test of your alertness.

As your Appointing Owner (remember he is no longer your client) has been champing at the bit for several weeks already, he is almost certainly going to get on with any works of demolition straight away. Demolition needs no notice *per se* (although if you are going to expose a party wall you will need to serve notice of that), but it can cause a lot of damage, and so it is essential to get the schedules of condition under way. As the named surveyor, you are probably above such petty matters, but you will have your juniors to do them for you.

Some surveyors think that it is the duty of the named surveyor to do every last little part of the proceedings himself. This might be true if the assistants they have to deal with have no authority from 'the surveyor' to make any decisions, and must report every last detail for higher judgment. However, if 'the surveyor' sends out assistants who are not only permitted to use, but are also capable of using, their own judgment, and provided that the big man (see note on gender on page xi) will always involve himself in any situation whose gravity demands it, then devolution is perfectly proper. The Pyramus & Thisbe Club debated delegation at one meeting, and decided that while Third Surveyor duties should never be passed down the line to the third assistant, it was quite in order for almost all other work to be carried out by juniors. It was agreed, though, that the named surveyor should acquaint himself at least superficially with every wall being dealt with, and take responsibility for any decisions or actions taken by his subordinates. If you honestly feel that your position demands that you should take every schedule yourself, don't be surprised if the surveyor on the other side does not guarantee to meet you personally on site – but sends competent juniors. Also don't be surprised if he refuses to agree the payment of principals' fees for juniors' work.

There are two schools of thought about how to agree schedules of condition. One school likes to go around with its opposite number and agree everything on the spot; the other prefers to take the schedule alone, and then send it to the other surveyor (or his assistant) for comments. Then there are two schools of thought about how actually to record the condition. One school favours writing it all down (and perhaps typing it up later); the other prefers a tape recorder. A third school (which we forgot to include in the first two) likes to take photographs, but despite developments in photography since the last edition of this book, they are still not really a substitute for description. Pyramus & Thisbe Club correspondence has also debated the use of video, which is now legally acceptable as evidence. However, it is not the legality which is troublesome in this instance, but the accuracy. One correspondent, for example, produced two photographs, taken a few moments apart, in which a crack was either millimetres or inches wide, depending on which photo you believed. But to sum up, it doesn't really matter how you do it, as long as it serves its purpose, which is to help to identify any damage caused by the works.

Eventually, the schedule is reduced to writing (or electronic text), and, after it has gone backwards and forwards a couple of times, you will have an agreed schedule.

Now, or more probably meanwhile, you can get down to discussing the physical impact of your proposals (let's call them yours, for simplicity) upon the adjoining property. Are there special precautions needed in any respect? Is it a bank, with vibration alarms in the walls? Is it a restaurant, which would be closed by the public health authorities if dirt and dust started flying? What's the basic user: domestic or commercial? Will the structure stand what is proposed for it? Will it need underpinning? Thickening? The flues blocked off? Will the party wall need to be more firmly fixed to the adjoining premises before your building is taken down? All these and more are practical questions which form the real meat of the party wall surveyor's activities.

From time to time, though not in the general run of cases, more serious questions may arise, such as whether the wall is a party wall at all, or whether you have the right to carry out the works proposed. The first of these you have no power to deal with, as it relates to title, which is a matter for the parties and their lawyers, but your advice and judgment should be the cornerstone of their proceedings. In fact, it was recently held by a judge hearing an appeal against a Third Surveyor's award that the latter had been quite correct to decide who owned a wall before making his award accordingly. He said that it would have been entirely proper for the Third Surveyor to have refrained from acting until the parties had obtained a legal decision, but equally right to make a decision and act on it, as his award was open to appeal. Of course, party wall surveyors are always deciding whether a wall is a party wall or not, and that they certainly can do on the basis of clear-cut evidence. Sometimes, however, there is no evidence, or it's wildly conflicting, and the parties are already at loggerheads over the ownership of the disputed piece of property. Then the surveyors are gazumped.

The following story illustrates this point. A very distinguished surveyor came to John, the Third Surveyor in this case, to decide just such a question. A notice had been served on his client/Appointing Owner (you will see the reason for the alternatives in a moment) purporting to initiate work to a party wall. The distinguished surveyor was of the opinion that it wasn't a party wall at all. After some to-ing and fro-ing, he and the bowler-hatted architect who claimed to be the Building Owner's Surveyor came to John for a decision. John put his findings in a letter, not an award, saying that in his opinion it was not a party wall, so that they were not appointed under what is now section 10, and that neither was John himself, so that his decision was not under the Act. This had two consequences, the first of which was that nobody paid John. The second was that the architect is reported to have returned to the attack on the Adjoining Owner, saying: 'Mr Anstey says he is not a properly appointed Third Surveyor. Therefore his opinion is not binding. Therefore I say it is a party wall'. (Only if it had been, John's decision that it wasn't would have been binding!) The end result, in case you're wondering, was that the Adjoining Owner threatened legal action if the Building Owner attempted to proceed under non-existent party wall rights, and the Building Owner sensibly abandoned those proposals.

As to whether the Building Owner has the right to carry out certain works or not, if you cannot decide between yourselves, you can turn to the Third Surveyor for judgment, and if the Appointing Owners don't like his or your decision they can appeal. But this is to anticipate ourselves. Let us return to the run-of-the-mill case.

In such a case, the next step is to draw up your award. We deal elsewhere with the detail of doing so[1], so you

---

[1] See Chapter 6.

can look there for advice on that. What we have just been talking about is the crucial and variable part of an award: the works which the Building Owner wants to carry out, and the requirements he must meet if he is to be allowed to do so.

In our run of the mill case, the Building Owner's Surveyor sends his draft award to the Adjoining Owner's Surveyor. In this new technological world, draft awards are often dispatched, and amended, by e-mail – without so much as a sheet of paper, photocopier or fax machine in sight. Often, but not always: many leading firms continue to work with hard copy. However it is done, the Adjoining Owner's Surveyor will indicate his amendments on the draft award, then either photocopy or otherwise 'save' his amended draft, and send the original back to his opposite number. After a little more to-ing and fro-ing on certain items, a fair copy of the final award can be produced and copies duly made of that: at least two copies for the parties, and one each for the surveyors.

Sometimes, lucky you, two interests in the property will agree to be bound by the same award. Then all you have to do is change the names and addresses a little and there is a completely different (?) final award.

All this happens, theoretically, before any work is done which needs the authorisation of the award. Sometimes even in practice it happens like that – although it is not unknown for awards to be finalised long after a building is up and occupied. Very often, when the two surveyors are men who know and trust each other, the official document may lag behind the works, although everything that is done affecting the Adjoining Owner will have been agreed as they went along. This is not, however, to be taken as approved practice. Technically, the Adjoining Owner is entitled to his award, and there are not a few surveyors who, whatever the standing of their opposite number or his Appointing Owner, will not allow a brick to be touched until the award has been delivered, their fees paid, and the days for appeal have run.

Strictly speaking, unless the award specifically allows for those 14 days for appeal to elapse before work may begin, the Building Owner can get cracking at once, but if there were to be an appeal after work had started, but within the days of grace, it might have unfortunate consequences. Most Third Surveyors would uphold the inclusion of a 14-day clause. The courts are unlikely to be happy if the possibility of an appeal is overlooked, either intentionally or accidentally. Note that in any case, the surveyors cannot shorten the period of notice in their award. Even if, *mirabile dictu*, everything proceeds with extreme rapidity, the earliest date on which work can start is two months (usually) after notice has been served – unless the Adjoining Owner himself consents to an earlier commencement.

Assuming once again, that we are following a normal sort of job, we may now at last let the Building Owner loose upon the party wall. We deliver his copy of the award to him (we've already extracted the Adjoining Owner's fees, so he'll be doubly anxious to be off) and, if we're prudent, draw his special attention to any particular requirements of which he may be unaware. It's also a good idea (in Graham's opinion – although this flatly contradicts John's earlier view) to tell one's Appointing Owner of his right of appeal. Note that this is by no means the same as encouraging him to exercise this; very rarely is such a thing even remotely justified, and it certainly isn't going to be so in our typical case. However, the evidence suggests that there is far more risk of a successful appeal out of time if the owner wasn't advised fully of his rights earlier on. Some distinguished authorities suggest writing a letter saying something like: 'You should be advised that you have a right of appeal to the County Court should you feel that there is anything in the award which should not be there, but I can assure you that I know of no reason for you to do so, since all your rights are fully protected therein'. John would still not agree, of course.

It is going to be important to make sure that the award is safely delivered to the hands of the owner, and does not lie around either surveyor's office until the end of the job. Many amateurs do not realise the importance of delivery, but as the right of appeal runs until 14 days after delivery, it is obviously essential that those days should start to run as soon as possible after the award is signed. Although, under the Arbitration Acts, time runs from when the arbitrator announces that his award is ready, it was held in *Gyle-Thompson v Walstreet*[1] that it didn't start until the Adjoining Owner had the thing in his possession. Finally, you need to impress upon the Building Owner how important it is that the contractor should be aware of his obligations under the award, and then again, you sit back and wait.

What you are waiting for this time is trouble. (We won't mention the sort when the Adjoining Owner's Surveyor – the sort who wants everything signed, sealed and delivered before the first sod is turned – goes on site and finds that half the work has been done already, when the

---

[1] See Chapter 16.

ink on the award is not yet dry.) The architect amends his plans, the engineer alters the foundations, the contractor ignores his instructions and, worst of all, the Building Owner changes his identity[1]. All these may require renegotiation with the Adjoining Owner's Surveyor, and some of them may require service of new notices, in which case remember that a new appointment of surveyors is required[2]. New awards may be needed, but if they are only to approve variations in the works, there should be little trouble about them. Many surveyors welcome addendum awards as an opportunity substantially to enhance their fees, so they will be quite happy to enter into them[3].

Lesser sorts of trouble are quite easy to deal with. Physical damage to next-door's property is just a matter of having it put right. It would, of course, be even easier if the contractor simply got on and repaired it, but such a suggestion elicits a hollow laugh from most professionals. Reglazing a window therefore involves two owners, two surveyors, a contractor, a sub-contractor, an insurance adjuster, and a bill of hundreds (if you're lucky) of pounds, for something that would have cost half a crown[4] (or thereabouts) to mend.

Nevertheless, physical damage is generally easy to sort out. Despite the automatic denials of the contractor, responsibility is usually fairly easy to determine, and the costing of the making good is not generally very difficult. Surprising as it may seem, many party wall jobs are even

[1] See Chapter 11.
[2] *Gyle-Thompson*: see Chapter 16.
[3] This is not meant as a commendation.
[4] John originally wrote this 15 years after decimalisation, and the time to update it has been and gone.

carried through without causing any physical damage to the adjoining premises at all.

A little more trouble is frequently caused by noise, and the Building Owner's Surveyor often has to try to sort out such problems, which are not really within his remit. This is part of a wider issue, of course. If the surveyor regards himself throughout the progress of the works on site as a man whose duty it is to resolve all problems between the owners, walking a fine line between not allowing the Adjoining Owner to be put upon nor the Building Owner to be exploited, he can hardly go wrong, though he will often find himself doing more than the strict interpretation of his role would seem to require. The one essential, in the authors' opinion, if he is to fulfil these wider obligations properly, is to know, and to let his Appointing Owner know, when he is acting as a party wall surveyor with power to bind and when he is acting as an adviser only. To add to that, the owner should take both sorts of admonition as orders, and do what he is told – although sadly, not all owners show such a proper sense of deference to their surveyors.

When the works are completed, it is advisable, though by no means invariable, for a final inspection to take place, at which the schedule of condition is checked and any damage agreed, to be subsequently put right or paid for. Many people recommend positive action by the Building Owner's Surveyor to put this in motion, so as to secure a positive clearance from the Adjoining Owner for the Building Owner, who can, barring accidents, be sure that he has now disposed of all claims from neighbours. Of course, this involves the surveyor finding out from the Building Owner, his contractor, or his architect when the job has actually reached the stage at which no further involvement of the neighbour's property is likely. A positive end to the job also has the advantage that the Adjoining Owner's Surveyor can put away his file for ever, either at once or after the making good, while the Building Owner's Surveyor can cross one adjoining property off his list and, when he has eventually crossed them all off, at last put in his own final bill, advise his Appointing Owner that all party wall matters are now at an end (always excepting any latent damage[1]), and consign his own file to the basement, electronic archive or the dustbin. (The last is not seriously recommended, but the tricolon is such an effective rhetorical device.) Anyway, *la commedia è finita*.

* * * *

That was the situation seen from a Building Owner's Surveyor's point of view. It is, of course, perfectly possible that the Adjoining Owner may consent to the works, and then a lot of what has been said above will be superfluous. However, you still need to keep a careful eye on certain things. The responsibility of the Building Owner in no way disappears, and he may well want to have his surveyor (who will not be a 'party wall surveyor' in this case) take a schedule of condition. Furthermore, he will not be able to get the surveyors to agree minor changes to the works in progress: he will have to negotiate any changes with the Adjoining Owner direct, and the latter might dissent from any changes at any stage, which would bring the whole issue within the standard procedures. Sometimes, therefore, this consent

---

[1] As the cases of *Selby v Whitbread* and *Brace v SE Regional Housing Association* make clear (see Chapter 16), a Building Owner is not relieved of his common law responsibilities, so any latent damage which emerged would still fall to his charge.

may turn out to be a two-edged weapon. For small works, though, such as flashing or the insertion of damp-proof courses, it must surely be desirable.

And now we must put ourselves in the position of the Adjoining Owner's Surveyor.

* * * *

So there you are, sitting quietly in your office, when the phone rings. 'I'm told you know all about party walls', a voice will say. At this point you should make some modest response, nevertheless indicating that you have sufficient grasp of the subject to assist your interlocutor. 'I've just received a...' – and there will be a pause while the speaker finds the form, turns it the right way up, and reads from the top of it '...a Party Structure notice. What on earth is it all about? It says they're going to do works to my party wall'.

Two ways are open to you at this point. You can spend the next half-hour or, if you go to visit your Appointing Owner, two hours (as it always seems to take longer face to face) pointing out that if it is a party wall it isn't 'his', and if it is his, it isn't a party wall, and then giving a resumé of party wall law and procedure. Or you can opt for the other way in which (better far), you tell him not to worry about it; you'll deal with it all; he should send the papers along to you; all he needs to do is to write to the chap who served the notice, using the acknowledgement form if one is attached, saying that he dissents and that he has appointed you. You then dictate over the phone (or e-mail or fax) a letter on the lines of the RICS draft 'Surveyor's Appointment and Authority' letter from the *Party Wall Legislation and Procedure* guidance note (which he will get wrong, so you later send him a fair copy for him to sign) and tell him to send that to you with the papers. After that, assure him he has nothing to worry about and nothing to do until you send him the award.

Most anxious laymen will now be quite reassured and will leave everything in your hands. Some, though, will think they know better, and will attempt to tell you how you should make things difficult for the Building Owner, preventing him altogether from carrying out his schemes, or delaying him as long as possible. Once again two choices are before you. You can decline to act further, and throw the whole thing back at him, or you can take what may be regarded as the more professional approach and (in all seriousness) ignore him. You simply do your duty as a party wall surveyor and refuse to impede the Building Owner or his surveyor, unless they should try to do anything improper.

A certain Adjoining Owner once became very wrathful at what he regarded as his surveyor's wilful refusal to act as he should, constantly disobeying orders to be obstructive, and generally going his own sweet way. He rang up the RICS in high dudgeon, and complained bitterly. 'Never mind,' said the soothing young lady on the other end, 'I'll put you in touch with a really nice party wall surveyor, who'll sort out all your problems. His name's John Anstey.'

'John Anstey!' spluttered the chap on the other end of the phone. 'That's the *!*! I've got acting for me!'

Typically, however, a short word of explanation will be all that's needed to make the situation clear to your anxious enquirer, and three days later (if the owner has used first class post), the papers will be on your desk. Your first duty is to see that your owner's interests are protected, so you must assure yourself that he has dissented and that you have been properly appointed. It doesn't matter too much whether he has dissented if it really was a notice under sections 3 or 6, but not everybody will use the RICS forms of notice, and some others can be quite confusing. However, it is always helpful if dissent is explicitly expressed, as then everybody knows what is going on, and even who the parties and their respective surveyors are.

While you are checking the notice, you will obviously see whether the Building Owner or his surveyor has filled it in properly. Very often he won't have done so, and as it is in everybody's interests that the formalities should be correct, you should at once write pointing out any deficiencies, while stating that you have no objection to getting on with the mechanics of the affair, while the errors are being corrected and notices re-served. Most experienced party wall surveyors have encountered clients who have sought to make the most effective use of defective notices by not telling the opposition until the last possible moment of their error – say, when they're just about to start work. Such behaviour is deplorable – and you should say so, unless the Building Owner is also trying to get away with some skulduggery, and is therefore fully deserving of a little tit for tat.

It is usually greatly preferable to communicate with the other side at once. As you don't want to get on bad terms with the Building Owner's Surveyor at the outset, a letter pointing out errors has to be written tactfully. The reason that it is in your Appointing Owner's interests to get everything straight is that he is going to be given certain protection by the award. If the proceedings are a nullity because of a defect in the notice, then so will be the award and the benefits it affords.

Regrettably, not all Building Owners' Surveyors recognise that this is meant to be helpful. If you ring them up and tell them about defects in the notice, they have been known to accuse you of obstruction, whereas in fact you are attempting to assist them. Do not allow the curmudgeonly attitude of a few to deter you from acting as a proper party wall surveyor. And remember that everyone makes mistakes in notices from time to time. John once told another (almost as) eminent surveyor's Appointing Owners that he proposed to demolish their building. The other surveyor had great fun putting him right.

If everything is in order on the notice and the dissent, you may care to send a copy of your letter of appointment to the Building Owner's Surveyor, and ask to see his, particularly if he has signed the notices, when you will want to see his authority to do so, for the reason set out above.

Now you must agree upon a Third Surveyor. This is as much your duty as it is the Building Owner's Surveyor, so if he has not suggested anyone so far, you may send him a list of names to choose from[1], usually three. His agreement in writing upon one of them completes this exercise. A schedule of condition of your Appointing Owner's premises is usually one of the next steps. This is more for the Building Owner's protection, in fact, but

---

[1] See Chapter 1.

Adjoining Owners like to see it being done. It makes them feel that someone is taking an interest in them, and they think that the schedule is for their protection – which to some extent it is. (You may well find the RICS 'Specimen Schedule of Condition', provided in the *Party Wall Legislation and Procedure* guidance note, useful here.)

Meanwhile, you will be considering the proposed works and, in particular, whether they are permitted under the Act. It may be that you will need to point out that a wall the other side proposes to use is not, in your opinion, a party wall, or that the other side will be making use of works carried out by your owner, and so liable to pay a contribution under section 11(11). You will also be deciding whether there are structural details which go beyond your competence as a surveyor. At this point we should stress that straightforward questions should not be too much for you – or you shouldn't have accepted the appointment in the first place. However, if there are complicated engineering questions, your Appointing Owner will need expert advice. The engineer's fee will have to be covered in the award, so you must seek your opposite number's agreement that such advice is reasonably required, and that he will award payment of fees sufficient to cover the engineer's needs as well as your own.

You may have enough competence to tell whether any rights of light issues arise – or other easements. But even if you have, and therefore do not have to call in an independent consultant to deal with them, don't attempt to cover them in the award[1].

[1] See Chapter 14.

Read the draft award carefully, when the Building Owner's Surveyor sends it to you. Check that the works covered therein are those declared on the notice. Ensure that your Appointing Owner is protected against damage, and against noisy works at unnecessarily inconvenient times. Check that you have an unfettered right of entry to the Building Owner's premises to see that everything is being done in accordance with the award.

As soon as you have agreed all the documentation, and signed it, publish it to your Appointing Owner. This is his one legal chance to interfere with your actions, and he must be given it. Remember that you should advise him of his right to appeal – while by no means encouraging this (a fine line to tread)!

You may have nominated a number of visits during the course of the works as part of the justification of your fee. Do look in to see that all is well, even if you are not beset with constant cries for help. You will probably have to explain to your Appointing Owner that the award only regulates work to the party wall, and not elsewhere, and that the noise he is complaining of comes from well over on the other side of the site. Nonetheless, it is probably no bad thing to try to keep general noise levels down, in the interests of neighbourliness, and you may be lucky enough to have a Building Owner's Surveyor who thinks the same.

From time to time, damage may occur. Impress on your Appointing Owner that he should tell you about it at once. If he happens to have next door the one foreman in the country who believes in putting right any little bits of damage without argument, you may never need to do any more about it. However, it is far more likely that you will have to call in your opposite number to agree upon responsibility and making good.

At all costs, try to stop your owner from putting damage right and removing the evidence before any of the professionals involved have seen it – if your owner wishes to make a claim, that is. You do get the odd people who are happy to put right damage themselves, perfectly quietly and without making a claim, to keep relations with the neighbours on track. But such people are few and far between, in the authors' experience.

Try to find out when the works are coming to an end – you'll be extremely lucky if anyone bothers to tell you – and arrange to make a final inspection of your owner's premises. It's much more helpful if any damage at this late stage can be noted and discussed before the contractor leaves the job, even if it is going to be the Building Owner's responsibility towards the Adjoining Owner in the first place. There's no reason why you shouldn't help him to recover from the people who actually caused the damage and, who knows, it may even be more convenient to have the contractor put the damage right himself, particularly if it's external, such as mortar droppings, blocked drains or cracked roof coverings.

If a lot of damage has occurred, you may be justified in asking for an additional fee for dealing with it, and you may even need an addendum award, although an exchange of letters is usually all that is required. When the damage is all put right, and the final payments have been made, you can sit back and wait for the phone to ring again.

A quick note on boundaries and awards

You don't need to deal with easements as a party wall surveyor – but you will be dealing with boundaries. Although some surveyors baulk at the idea of it, party wall surveyors confirm the boundary position in almost every award they make. An award will normally say whether or not the wall is party, or where the line of junction is between properties. Remember, for a Building Owner to exercise rights under section 2, the wall must be party, either astride the boundary or by separating buildings. If the wall is described as a section 20(a) party wall, i.e. astride the boundary, then the surveyors are making a statement as to where the boundary lies.

One exception is an award dealing with works under section 2(2)(j), which allows for the chasing in of flashings to an Adjoining Owner's flank wall. Even in this case, though, the surveyors are confirming that next door's wall is owned by them.

If the boundary position is contentious between the owners, but surveyors feel they can deal with those issues arising from the notice and the matters covered by the Act, then they should make their award and publish it, highlighting to the owners the clause (or clauses) that address those contentious issues and informing them of their rights of appeal. If the owners do take exception, they can then appeal the award.

Surveyors could of course take the view that they should not deal with these issues. However, as long as they fall within the Act, it is the authors' view that they should.

5 Notice

There are two aspects to the matter of giving notice: how to do it, and how much to give. There is an easy answer to the first part: use the RICS forms for notice and acknowledgement provided in the *Party Wall Legislation and Procedure* guidance note. This isn't, however, what you might call the correct answer, to which we will at once turn.

There is no statutory form on which notice must be given – not the RICS one, not even that provided by the Pyramus & Thisbe Club in '*The Green Book*', and certainly not the RIBA (Royal Institute of British Architects) one. You will find that some people, semi-professionals rather than amateurs or real professionals, demand to receive a 'proper' notice, if you send them anything except a printed form. If your only wish is to appease them, then use a printed form. If not, then draw their attention to the words of the Act which are, in section 3 at least (and the words in section 1 and section 6 are like unto them) '...a building owner shall serve on any adjoining owner a notice...stating a) the name and address of the building owner; b) the nature and particulars of the proposed work...' and a lot of detail about special foundations again. Obsessed with special foundations, the authors of the Act were. The only requirement is for these particulars to be included – whether you write a letter or use a form. In addition, you must give the date on which it is intended to start work.

In the case of a notice under section 6 you must, as remarked on elsewhere, also include plans and sections, which is extraordinary, the extraordinariness lying in the fact that you aren't required to include them in a notice under section 3 unless special foundations (again!) are involved. (Why, you may wonder incidentally, without much hope of getting an answer, does the notice of works under section 2 get a section of its own, 3, while the one under section 6 has to be content with a sub-section, (5)?)

It cannot be wrong, and is certainly helpful to the recipient, to provide plans with your notice, whatever it concerns. Almost the first request an Adjoining Owner's Surveyor will make is to receive some, if they haven't already been sent to him.

Included in the information with your section 6 notice must be plans and sections showing the site and the depth to which you propose to excavate. It is not enough to say: pile depth to be decided on site. Funnily enough, no-one is likely to quibble if you change the intended depth, even quite drastically, and later substitute 50-foot piles for 20-foot ones, but they are very likely to reject your notice as inadequate if it mentions no depth at all.

We are coming to periods of notice shortly, but it should be noted at this stage that there are minima and maxima. It wouldn't be at all surprising if a court were to rule that a notice that purported to name a starting date outside the limits was completely void, and could not be validated simply by the amendment of the date. You must give the date on which you expect to start work; it must fall within the prescribed limits; and if, as so often happens, you have been instructed that the job is starting next week, while two months' notice is needed, you can only beg the Adjoining Owner's indulgence – not, be it noted, his surveyor's. In order to avoid silly errors of putting a date in for starting, and then forgetting to sign and send the notice for a couple of days, so that the starting date is now less than two months away, you can write 'as soon as notice has run', which cannot be incorrect.

Notice is only valid for 12 months, so you should avoid serving too early, but it must be admitted that the more usual problem is not having sufficient time before work starts to give the requisite period of notice. This is particularly true of 'Design and Build' contracts. The right combination of owner, plans and party wall surveyors rarely seems to come into existence more than a few days before the intended start on site. It is essential that as soon as the design and build route is decided upon, someone addresses the party wall problem, and tries to assemble the necessary information to enable notice to be served.

Hold on, you may be exclaiming. Who is serving the notice? Is it an owner or his surveyor? The answer is that (see above) the Building Owner must give notice, but his hand is usually being held by someone else. When John first began specialising in party walls, the Building Owner himself almost invariably signed the notices, even if he hardly knew what he was doing. In the face of considerable opposition at first, John gradually made it acceptable for the Building Owner's Surveyor, who understands far better what is needed in the notice, and who frequently did all but the signing in the past, to sign and serve the notices himself, provided he is armed with a suitable letter of authority from his principal, because in this case he is acting as the agent of the owner, not as his appointed surveyor. This is now so much the generally accepted practice that RICS publish a draft letter for giving that authority ('Surveyor's Appointment and Authority' in the *Party Wall Legislation and Procedure* guidance note).

An odd little problem that crops up sometimes is finding out who the Building Owner is. (It's also often hard to find out who the Adjoining Owner is, and we'll come to that shortly.) Under the complicated financial arrangements which seem to prevail these days, and which we have no intention of pretending to understand, the chap who is actually going to carry out the building works often doesn't have a legal interest (though he may have an equitable interest) in the site until the day before the works begin – if then. However, the Building Owner can't assign, in the opinion of the authors, the benefit of a notice which he has served on behalf of the incoming developer. The man who serves the notice must be the one who is going to do the building works (see the definition of Building Owner in Chapter 1) and he must be an owner within the definition given in the same section. Sometimes developers don't tell you that they don't actually own the site – it's wounding to their *amour propre* - and always talk as if they 'own' all the sites they're concerned with. They are also inclined not to inform you which of their subsidiaries is going to be the nominal owner, and you tend to find that out when you send them the award, and they send it back and ask you to change the name on it!

Always ask, at the outset, who has the legal ownership of the site and, if appropriate, which subsidiary is going to be involved. The Act does specifically recognise as an owner someone with a contract to purchase or an agreement for lease, so the incoming owner will have an interest before completion. If the result of these enquiries is that the 'wrong' person owns the site at present, then the only solution that springs to mind is to serve in the name of the present owner and, as soon as the 'new' owner has his interest, serve a new notice in the latter's name and ask the Adjoining Owner to waive the waiting period of a new notice.

Counsel has pointed out that the definition of owner 'includes' various categories. That means that it is not necessarily limited to those specifically mentioned, and the courts might well hold, therefore, that a building owner in possession of the site was the 'Building Owner' in the eyes of the Act. It may then be sufficient for such an owner to serve notice on his own. A purchaser under contract who hasn't yet entered into actual possession most certainly qualifies in this way. This doesn't, however, remove the necessity for finding out which name the developer is operating under.

Under the LBA, the actual service of the notice was covered by a section of whose existence many people were ignorant, namely 124, which also dealt with the problem of unknown Adjoining Owners. Now that the Act is much shorter, section 15, which deals with service, is likely to be better known. Notice must be delivered to the residence, place of business, or registered office of the Adjoining Owner, according to who is being served.

The Land Registry will be able to give you some, if not all, the names of the Adjoining Owners. Your notice can then be addressed only to those who have an interest in the adjoining property of greater than 12 months. It's always better, if possible, to address a letter and notice to an individual or a company.

If you can't find out who owns or occupies the premises, you can simply address your notice to 'the owner', naming the premises in question and delivering it. If you can't find anyone on the premises to hand it to, you must have it fixed 'to a conspicuous part of the premises'. It is so easy to comply that there can rarely be any excuse for failure to serve notice. In addition, it is a good idea always to accompany notices with a letter asking the recipient to let you know if he holds from anyone, or if anyone holds from him. This procedure is not infallible, however. John was once six months into a job before the borough council, whom he fondly believed to be the freeholders, informed him that they were only head leaseholders. Very occasionally, you may find that the same person or company owns more than one of the properties which adjoin the Building Owner's site. You need only serve one notice on that Adjoining Owner, though you must specify therein all of his properties that are going to be affected.

It's preferable and generally serves to create a better atmosphere if you can address the Adjoining Owner by name, so don't automatically take the easy way out and serve all your notices on 'the owner'. In any case, this may lead to difficulties if you serve one such notice on a property which turns out to be internally divided. Out of three 'owners', only one may receive the notice, and he may be the one who throws it in the wastepaper basket.

Try to identify as many Adjoining Owners as possible. It's always a good idea to start by asking your client – as you haven't served notice yet, he's still your client, not your Appointing Owner – what he knows about the ownership of next door. Often he will have been in contact with the surrounding properties for some reason or other, such as trying to buy them, and can let you know quite a lot about them. You can, of course, also go and read the name-plates on the door, if you're dealing with office buildings – or even ring the bell and ask.

The point of this, of course, is that notice must be given to all owners and, says the Act (to repeat the extract in Chapter 1), 'owner includes (a) a person in receipt of...the whole or part of the rents or profits...; (b) a person in possession of land, otherwise than as a mortgagee or as a tenant from year to year or for lesser term or as a tenant at will; (c) a purchaser of an interest...under a contract...or under an agreement for a lease...'. There can be almost as many 'owners' in a building as there are coffee beans in Brazil. As with Building Owners, these may be people with not very obvious equitable interests, either as purchasers under a contract or lessees under an agreement for lease. One vexed question, not yet satisfactorily settled, is whether a holding-over tenant has an interest which comes within the definition. Some surveyors, quoting an analogous decision in a valuation case, hold that he does. Others, applying logic, say that he doesn't. Be warned that he might.

Several surveyors have suggested that more could be said about this subject, but the truth is that we need a good leading case or two to determine whether these equitable interests qualify their holders as Owners, Building or

Adjoining. A reliable informant says that the answer as to whether a holding-over tenant is an owner is that immortal response: yes and no. True holding-over arises from periodical tenancies or from the effluxion of a fixed term tenancy. The first gives rise to a similar periodic holding, and the second to a tenancy from year to year: neither of these qualifies as ownership. In the case of an expired business tenancy, however, the tenant can go on occupying virtually for ever, unless the tenancy is brought to an end by one of the means envisaged by the *Landlord and Tenant Act* 1954. This latter kind of holding-over tenant probably therefore is an owner.

Virtually no council tenants are owners, and the authors maintain that you do not need to give notice to mortgagees. John's practice (with which Graham concurs) was not to rely upon the Building Owner's doubtful standing when serving notice on his behalf, and to assume that a tenant in occupation might well rank as an owner, whatever his status. Both authors agree that in the latter case it is probably better to serve in haste and repent at leisure.

Then there is the bicycle shed against Dolphin Square problem (Dolphin Square used to be the biggest block of flats in Europe). Upon how many of the owners do you have to serve notice if your proposed building affects only a small piece of wall? The question quite often seriously arises in blocks of offices where, say, a top floor is being added to a block which has a party wall with another building in multi-occupation. Certainly you must include the freeholder (and any long leaseholders) and the occupier immediately adjoining the works, but what about those lower down (or sometimes further up) the same wall? The authors would suggest that, strictly speaking, unless their demise includes the part of the wall being worked on, they are not entitled to notice. However, if their bit of wall might be affected by settlement or any other disturbance transmitted through the wall, either upwards or downwards, then it would probably be wise to include them in the service. There are other ways of dealing with Adjoining Owners besides serving notice, if you think that one is not legally required. You can write a friendly, neighbourly letter saying what you intend to do, and you can even take a schedule of condition without being governed by the Act.

There are a number of counter-notices referred to in the Act. Occasionally, people even serve them. Sometimes, even the right people. The Act requires the owner to serve the counter-notice, and his surveyor can only do so if specifically authorised. The term can probably be extended to cover all formal letters of response, whether they are so described by the Act or not. The first to be so mentioned, though not a counter-notice as such, is a consent in writing to a proposal to erect a party wall or party fence wall at joint expense, under section 1(3).

Consent in writing is always necessary for a proposal to use reinforced concrete foundations on an Adjoining Owner's land, and consent from the owner at that, not his surveyor. If the Adjoining Owner gives explicit consent in response to any notice, section 3(3)(a) makes it clear that the procedures of section 10 are not necessary.

The counter-notice proper follows immediately after, in section 4. This lists two 'positive' kinds of dissent, if that makes any sense. These are not actually dissents from the proposed works, but ask for more to be added unto them. If the Building Owner is proposing to carry out work to a party structure, the Adjoining Owner can require him to build in chimney breasts, piers, and the like, for his convenience, while if he is consenting to special foundations, he can ask for them to be deeper or stronger so that he can use them.

No counter-counter-notice is required. Silence to a section 4 counter-notice has the same effect as silence to a section 3 notice: it produces deemed dissent after 14 days.

No notice is necessary if works have to be carried out under a Dangerous Structure notice (section 3(3)(b)), while for gaining access to adjoining premises, although 14 days is normally necessary, in an emergency only as much notice 'as may be reasonably practicable' needs to be given.

Although there are periods of notice mentioned in section 10, they are of a different nature, and we have left them to another, shorter, chapter[1]. It is necessary, however, to deal with the question of how long a period of notice is needed in the sections we have covered. A table is probably the simplest and clearest way to show this, and we duly end the chapter with this. Note, however, that not all notices require the same kind of response.

[1] See Appendix III.

Section	Works	Period of notice
1(2)	Building a party wall	1 month
1(5)	Building a wall on his own land	1 month
1(6)	Placing foundations on Adjoining Owners' land	More than 1 month and less than 12 months
3	Any works to a party fence wall, special foundations, or any works to a party structure	2 months
[Note: all works specified under section 3 must be begun within 12 months.]		
4(2)	Counter-notice re special foundations or other matters	1 month
5	Consent to a notice under section 3	14 days
6(5)	Building within 3 or 6 metres	More than 1 month and less than 12 months
6(7)	Consent to 6(3)	14 days
8(4)	Entering adjoining premises	14 days or as much notice as can be given in the case of an emergency

Preparation of an award

It is a lot easier nowadays to prepare an award than it used to be. There are basically two forms in common use, one of them more common than the other, so we'll deal with the latter first. It begins:

AWARD

IN THE MATTER OF

THE PARTY WALL etc. ACT 1996

To all to whom these presents shall come we S. Bailey, FRICS of 13, St Bartholomew's Street, EC1 in the County of London, and L. Cole, FRICS of 31, Quoin Street, St Bartholomew's, EC1 in the County of London

SEND GREETING

Whereas M. D'Souza and Company of such and such an address hereinafter called the Building Owners are the owners of premises known as somewhere or other.

And whereas S. Taylor and Company of another address hereinafter called the Adjoining Owners are the owners of premises known as something else.

AND WHEREAS the Building Owners desire to exercise the rights given to them under the Party Wall etc. Act, 1996, notice whereof was served on the Adjoining Owners on or about the 16th day of May 2004.

AND WHEREAS a dispute has been deemed to have arisen between the Building Owners and the Adjoining Owners.

AND WHEREAS the Building Owners have appointed the said S. Bailey to act as their Surveyor and the Adjoining Owners have appointed the said L. Cole to act as their Surveyor.

AND WHEREAS the said two Surveyors have selected Sir Edgar Horne, PPRICS of Another World as Third Surveyor and agree that in the event of his being unable to act and their not jointly deciding upon a substitute another Third Surveyor shall be appointed by the Appointing Officer.

The other sort starts rather more prosaically:

Whereas M. D'Souza and Company of such and such an address (hereinafter referred to as the Building Owners) owners of the premises known as such and such did on the 29th day of February Two Thousand and Four serve upon S. Taylor and Company (hereinafter referred to as the Adjoining Owners) owners within the meaning of the Act of the adjoining premises known as such and such, notice of their intention to exercise the rights given to them under the Party Wall etc. Act, 1996, Section 6, by executing works as more particularly defined in the notice.

It, too, then deals with the appointment of surveyors, and goes on something like this:

Now we, being two of the three Surveyors so appointed, having inspected the said premises, DO HEREBY AWARD AND DETERMINE as follows:

1. (a) That such and such address is an adjoining building standing close or adjacent to the boundary.

    (b) That the building is sufficient for the present purposes of the Adjoining Owners.

    (c) That the condition of the fourth floor of the building is as described in the schedule of condition dated such and such attached hereto and forming part of this award.

    (d) That drawing nos. such and such attached hereto and signed by us the said two Surveyors form part of this award.

These are really only the preambles. The meat of the award follows, in which the works are set out, together with the manner of their execution.

Many examples of this latter type in fuller form can be found, but particularly readily in the RICS guidance note, *Party Wall Legislation and Procedure*. (The same award is provided in the RICS *Party Wall Legislation and Procedure – Notices and Letters* CD-ROM, with the advantage that it can be copied and re-used electronically in this format.) On the assumption that you have already bought (or at the worst, are going to buy) the RICS guidance note or CD-ROM, no sample is produced here. Instead, we will concentrate on the two aspects of producing a final document, which are, firstly, drawing up a satisfactory draft and secondly, getting it agreed.

Before that, however, it is worth just mentioning the school of thought which holds that surveyors are simple, straightforward practical men, not complicated devious chaps like lawyers, and that their awards should therefore eschew all flowery pseudo-legal language, and read thus:

On 11th October, M. D'Souza ('the Building Owner') served a notice on S. Taylor ('the Adjoining Owner') under Section 46(1)(e), about the building at 100, Whiteacre Street, EC1.

S. Taylor dissented from the notice and appointed as his Surveyor S. Bailey of 13, St Bartholomew's Street, EC1.

M. D'Souza then appointed as his Surveyor L. Cole of 31, Quoin Street, EC1.

The two Surveyors selected as Third Surveyor Sir E. Horne of Another World, and so on.

While this style has a certain naive charm, it hasn't caught on yet. However, an award in this form should be equally effective in fact and in law.

On now to the practical aspects of producing an award – leaving it to you to choose whichever style of presentation you prefer. (We would emphasise, though, that it is advisable, especially if you are a beginner, to follow a reliable draft at least the first few times you try to prepare an award. It's all too easy to miss out something essential if you try to write your own version from scratch.)

The first page or so of the award will deal with 'recitals', that is to say the sort of information illustrated above, and it should be a straightforward record of fact: the names and addresses of the owners; the names of their surveyors; the Third Surveyor; the addresses of the properties concerned (not necessarily the same as the addresses of the owners in commercial cases, although usually so in domestic ones); the date of notice; the type of notice (party structure, three metre or six metre); and/or the sections under which it was served.

The next thing to do is to state the basic nature of the structure/s you are dealing with. Is it a party wall, or are there two independent buildings? State which. Say whether the wall serves the needs of the Adjoining Owner adequately: this will help to explain any apportionment of costs. Record the taking of a schedule of condition if one has been taken (and if not, why not?). Formally incorporate it in the award, and do the same for any drawings you propose to attach to the award.

A word about drawings. Most awards have too many drawings attached. In the good old days (that is to say, pre-1939), most awards were accompanied by 'party wall drawings' showing precisely, and often showing only, the relationship between the Building Owner's and the Adjoining Owner's buildings, in plan and section on one or two sheets. Nowadays, a combination of architect's, engineer's and the odd party wall drawing are used, frequently unselectively, so that bundles of ten or more drawings may be involved. Not only does this make the award document ridiculously bulky, but it also makes the lay Appointing Owner far less likely or able to appreciate what is involved. In addition, it tires out the poor surveyor who must sign all the drawings.

It is therefore sensible to limit the number of drawings to be attached to the award to the bare minimum. That does not mean that the Adjoining Owner's Surveyor should not possess a full set, but only that they are not all necessary in the final document. You may, as implied above, still need to produce a drawing specifically for the award, or have it produced by the architects. There may be abutment or flashing details which are inadequately covered elsewhere, and which are of more import and interest to the Adjoining Owner and his surveyor than the make of lift or the type of ironmongery.

Care needs to be taken when including in an award drawings that detail construction not covered by that award. For example, an award may deal with foundations, but the drawings could include superstructure works which still need to be agreed. Confusion has reigned in such instances, so it is important to be meticulous when confirming which drawings should be attached.

Having said all of that, if an award covers really extensive works, for example under sections 1, 2 and 6, then sometimes there will be many drawings attached – perfectly legitimately. In these situations, a document register listing all the drawings, schedules of condition and method statements can be signed by the surveyors, avoiding the need to sign every drawing and document. The drawings are still attached to the award and form part of it, with the document register being referred to in the main text of the award.

Having addressed the matter of the drawings, it is now vital at this juncture to differentiate between the works that the Building Owner *wishes* to do, and those that he *must* do, for the protection of the Adjoining Owner, if he implements the former. This was the nub of *Marchant v Capital and Counties*[1], but the gist of the Court of Appeal's decision was that all works referred to in the award which may be necessary for the good of the Adjoining Owner must be carried out by the Building Owner, once he decides to proceed with his works, and that in the event of any ambiguity (and, it is suggested, even in the face of a plain contrary meaning) in the wording of the award, it will be construed in favour of the Adjoining Owner.

You must be careful to put into the clause concerning works which the Building Owner *wishes* to do all those things for which he needs the power of the Act. There is no right to do more than is stated, or to infer more than is stated: he can only do what is written down. It is usual, indeed, to add that no material deviation from the stated works shall be permitted without express agreement (although section 7(5) explicitly states that there shall be no deviation from the plans).

It is also worth stating that the Building Owner is under no obligation to carry out his own works. You won't be thanked for binding him to proceed with a major development when his financial circumstances are causing him to hesitate before starting.

Now you can turn to those things which are a condition of the Building Owner being allowed to do what he wants. These are fairly standard, and are listed in the RICS draft award, but there may obviously be specific requirements for a particular job: a problem of support;

[1] For a full discussion of this case, see Chapter 16.

attention to vibration alarms in the wall of a bank; or filters for air conditioners; or the shuttering off of part of the adjoining premises in order to allow the demolition of the party wall. It is usual to specify at this point whether access to the Adjoining Owner's property is necessary for carrying out the works, or even that it is to be avoided. Section 8 will give you the right of access if it is needed[1].

The rights of access of the two surveyors must also be covered. It is usual to give the Adjoining Owner's Surveyor a much more free hand than the Building Owner's Surveyor. There is usually no good reason why the former should not be allowed on to the site at any time when work is going on, to see that his Appointing Owner's rights are being respected, and it is equally reasonable that the Building Owner's Surveyor should have to give notice (or make an appointment) if he wants to come on to occupied premises to inspect something.

Hours of working are often specified – or at least of noisy working. This can lead to acrimonious discussion, especially in mixed company. It is easy enough, provided you are prepared to put up with restrictions at all, to agree to limit working to suit one class of Adjoining Owner – office, shop or domestic – but when all three are closely entwined, there is no hour of the day or night when one of them will not want you to be silent. On the whole, the courts are more generous in allowing hours of noisy working than Adjoining Owners' Surveyors, so you could always threaten recourse to them, if you are the Building Owner's Surveyor. However you settle the matter, here's the place in the award to do so.

---

[1] See Chapter 9.

It is usual to say (but probably unnecessary) that the works should be in accordance with any other statutory requirements and the Act[1]. It is more necessary to say that the works must proceed without undue delay, and to put in a time limit for their completion. An award is not a perpetual licence to a Building Owner to interfere with the property of his neighbours. It may be necessary, and it is certainly usual, to reserve the right for the surveyors to make further awards arising out of the works as necessary, although in the authors' opinion, the duty placed upon the surveyors by section 10(10) to 'settle by award any matter (a) which is connected with any work to which this Act relates, and (b) which is in dispute...' clearly gives them such power, whether the first award specifically says so or not.

Fees for the Adjoining Owner's Surveyor are usually, but not quite invariably, set down in the award[2], and some surveyors refuse to sign or hand over the award until they see the colour of the Building Owner's money. John always regarded this as unprofessional, however, and only did so if he had been jilted more than once by the same man. Graham concurs. Technically, it might also be correct for the Building Owner's Surveyor's fees to be laid down in the award, and the responsibility for them placed upon the appropriate owner (which might well be the Building Owner!) but it is seldom, if ever, done[3].

The last effective clause usually found in an award was much debated by an RICS working party before its inclusion was agreed. This clause points out that an

[1] Sometimes even planning consent is included.
[2] More about fees in Chapter 7.
[3] Noel Coward.

award does not override easements of light or others in a party wall, and virtually repeats the gist of section 9. For that reason, its mention is unnecessary, but its inclusion was agreed because the owner who gets the award is probably not familiar with section 9, and this spelling out reassures the layman that his rights in such respects are unaffected.

You should now have a draft award which needs no amending, but it is a rare bird indeed which returns to the ark without some additional feathers stuck in by the other surveyor. Moreover, while draft awards are usually drawn up by the Building Owner's Surveyor, this is not invariably the case. If you, a knowledgeable, experienced, Adjoining Owner's party wall surveyor (which you will be by the time you've waded through all this, even if you weren't already) find yourself dealing with an innocent architect who has suddenly been called upon to grapple with the intricacies of the Act as a Building Owner's Surveyor, it will often be a positive kindness to both of you to relieve him of the attempt to write his first award from first principles[1], and send him one of your own.

Let us assume the more usual circumstances. As the Building Owner's Surveyor, you are certainly better placed to describe the intended works and it is only reasonable that most of the burden of producing an award should fall upon you. You now send it to your opposite number. Theoretically, he has ten days to act upon it[2], but he may well need some urging to get on with it: his owner isn't champing at the bit, waiting to proceed with the works. Theoretically, if he doesn't reply within ten days after a

[1] Which you were warned against a few pages ago.
[2] See Appendix III.

written request to do so, the first surveyor can proceed *ex parte*, but this is a course which is usually only taken as a last resort. Instead, the Building Owner's Surveyor writes increasingly urgent letters as his Appointing Owner writes him increasingly aggressive ones – demanding to know when he's going to get signed awards.

If you are the Adjoining Owner's Surveyor it is your duty to respond promptly to the receipt of a draft award. Apart from anything else, you are putting your Appointing Owner at risk of an *ex parte* award, and so you should deal with any points of disagreement in the draft and send it back. It is often helpful to discuss these on the telephone, so that what you are sending back are, in effect, agreed amendments. These should preferably be written in different coloured ink on the draft (or indicated clearly electronically), so that the other surveyor can immediately identify them. This process should normally only take one exchange of documents and one telephone call. Very often, you may prefer a slightly different method of wording some clause or other, but it's not really productive to be pedantic about things like that. As long as principles are unaffected, let it go.

The same goes for the Building Owner's Surveyor when he gets the award back. If the other chap's amendments don't really affect the basic working of the award, why bother to quibble? Have the thing fair copied (or the electronic equivalent), and made up into a nice document with its accompanying drawing (that's just a pious hope for the singular) and schedule.

When it comes to the final document, we have to deal with the date and the signatures. You wouldn't think that people could get this wrong, but they do. The document is not effective until the second man signs – it is not the first signatory who dates the document, therefore, but the second.

The named surveyor should, of course, actually sign in the presence of the person who is going to add his name as witness. You should be meticulous about this, to the extent of stopping signing if the witness is called out of the room for any reason – such as going to fetch a pen! But not everyone is so scrupulous. It is not even unknown – occasionally – to receive 'witnessed' awards lacking the surveyor's signature. While best legal advice suggests that the witnessing is not, strictly speaking, legally necessary, it can be highly desirable. If it's going to be done at all, it should be done properly.

The witness should be of legal age, and should give his personal address, which is not that of the office, unless he happens to be a principal of the firm. John used to write back to such offenders congratulating them on having a living-in secretary, or on having made some junior a partner. Contrary to what some may think, it is perfectly proper for a wife to witness a husband's signature on an award, or vice versa.

Finally, the surveyor should sign the schedule of condition and all the drawings and perhaps date them. These do not need to be witnessed.

Really finally, the completed award should be promptly despatched to the respective owners (section 10(14)), so that the period for appeal can begin to run as soon as possible after the award is complete, as both parties are bound by the award if no appeal is made.

That was really finally, until this book ran into several editions, and thus into another couple of paragraphs. Bear with us – you must be able to see the end of the page by this point.

It is, of course, perfectly possible, and often desirable, to have more than one award on a job. Quite often, the Building Owner will not have details of the superstructure available when he wants to get on with the foundations. It will probably cost him more in fees, but save him even more in time (and therefore money), if he asks his surveyor to produce what may be called a 'Foundation Award', to be followed in due course by a 'Superstructure Award'. Sometimes even these two are not enough, and may be preceded by a 'Demolition Award'. Very often, this last is a legal fiction, as the Building Owner does not need its sanction to make his activities legal, but it helps to establish the relationship between the parties and produces an agreed schedule of condition which has all the air of being legally binding. While the authors would not discourage the use of such 'awards', it is wise to heed a mild word of caution against relying too heavily upon one, if faced with an Adjoining Owner intent upon exploiting every loophole.

The question is often asked as to when an award comes to the end of its effectiveness. Before *Marchant v Capital and Counties*[1], it could have been argued that it ceased to apply as soon as all making good was completed at the end of the works covered in the award. However, in *Marchant* the Court of Appeal made a ruling implying that in some circumstances an award could run indefinitely. John always considered this a bad ruling –

[1] See Chapter 16.

and the wrong one on the facts – noting that in the majority of cases the award would still die with the end of the building contract next door or, at the latest, soon after. You should also bear in mind that the Adjoining Owner will still have his common-law rights if some unforeseen catastrophe should strike him at a later date.

7 Fees

How on earth can you write about fees, when they're going to have changed their value as soon as a book is published? You can't, of course, but you can offer general guidance. (You might also find Chapter 10, 'Who pays for what?' useful.)

Circumstances are completely different for surveyors depending on whether they're acting for Building Owners or Adjoining Owners. A job for a Building Owner will be taken on a time charge basis. You can give an estimate, if feasible, and can quote the hourly rates which you will charge, but you should not tie yourself to a fixed sum. You cannot possibly tell, when a job begins, whether the contractor will make for a smooth and happy relationship with all the neighbours, or whether you will constantly have to be dashing down to the site to clear up after damage – metaphorically speaking. An Adjoining Owner's Surveyor, though, will usually calculate an overall fee for the job as a whole (see below).

Different rates should be charged for different grades of staff. It should be remembered, however, that in specialised firms, even juniors will be extremely knowledgeable and experienced in party wall matters, so rates should apply to levels of knowledge and experience, and not simply age or length of service in the firm.

Travelling time can be a bone of contention. For a central London firm dealing with central London jobs, it hardly matters; their surveyors will quite frequently visit two or three jobs in one outing. There are provincial firms though (in the Home Counties, as well as further afield) who take on party wall work in London and want to be paid for three hours' travelling time on each site inspection as well as being reimbursed at metropolitan rates for their time spent on site. On the other side of the coin, there are London firms who take on work in distant parts of the country, and not only want to be paid their usual metropolitan rates, but also for their travelling time and costs. Unless it is a very specialist matter requiring the sort of top class expertise for which it is always right and proper to pay extra, such charges cannot really be justified. More than one such claim has been taken to the Third Surveyor. If offered work in distant parts for Adjoining Owners, surveyors should either fit their visits in with other business in the area, or else pass the work on to someone else in the first place. If neither of these courses is open to them, then they should charge either moderately or not at all for travelling.

You should not charge principal's fees for doing a junior's work. It is not always easy, of course, to decide what constitutes work demanding a partner's time and attention, and what can safely be left to juniors, but the effort must be made in all but one-man-bands. It is perfectly acceptable, as noted previously in this book, for the vast bulk of the work to be done by capable assistants, and it is in everyone's interest that it should be so, not least that of the man who is footing the bills.

The Act states that the **reasonable** costs of making an award, for reasonable inspections and any other matter arising out of the notice, shall be paid. In the majority of cases, the Building Owner is responsible for paying these fees, although it is for the surveyors to decide this.

The surveyor should keep this concept of 'reasonableness' in mind when proposing a fee. Sometimes it is not necessary for an Adjoining Owner's Surveyor to undertake an interim inspection, yet the proposed fee allows for one. If the works are minor (see the end of this chapter), there is no need to spend lots of hours in making the award, nor is an interim inspection necessary.

If a dispute concerning fees is dealt with by the Third Surveyor, then his fees have to be paid as well. He may decide to award these against one party or split them between the owners[1]. Either way, the added costs often exceed the original fee claimed and the referral normally results in a delay to the works starting. This is not a healthy situation and creates bad feeling between neighbours, particularly in residential situations. If a reference to the Third Surveyor is necessary, it should be done as quickly and succinctly as possible, so that the issue does not drag on.

At least the Building Owner's Surveyor's fee charging is comparatively simple, even if his position as agent, adviser or arbitrator[2] is not always clearly defined: at the end of the job he tots up the hours and bills his client/Appointing Owner accordingly. The Building Owner has complete control over whom he appoints, at least at the outset (although if he changes his opinion about his surveyor, he can't change his appointment). If he wants to appoint the man in the moon and pay his

[1] See Chapter 8.
[2] See Appendix IV.

travelling expenses to monthly site meetings, that's up to him. The Adjoining Owner's Surveyor, however, is thrust upon him, and that's when the Building Owner's Surveyor has to protect his Appointing Owner by resisting claims for extortionate sums.

It is only reasonable that the Adjoining Owner's Surveyor should be asked to calculate an overall fee for the job as a whole, given a fairly normal progression from notice to completion. By the time he inserts the figure in the award, a lot of the work will already have been done, and the scope of the work will certainly be clear. He can always protect himself against unforeseen complications by careful wording of the award[1]. However, a certain amount of guesswork has to be undertaken, and some people are rather notorious for the high level of their guesses. This is not fair on the Building Owner, nor is it a professional attitude to one's job. Make a reasonable estimate, and hope for swings as well as roundabouts, or vice versa.

Slightly more problematic is the question of how to charge for an Adjoining Owner's unreasonableness. If he constantly drags you down to the site, wrongly alleging that work to the party wall has started or that damage has been caused, should such visits be charged to the Building Owner? In equity, they certainly should not, but there's little hope of recovering fees for them from your Appointing Owner. The sort who call you out at the least provocation are just the sort who will most strongly resist the suggestion that they should pay for it. One solution, by no means perfect, is to send them a note of your fees – but not by way of a VAT account – telling them that you will send such an account when the fee is paid. You may

[1] See the last few pages of Chapter 4.

also be able to square it with your conscience to charge half the fee to the Building Owner, if the Adjoining Owner does not pay you.

More and more disputes in recent years have concerned the Adjoining Owner's Surveyors' fees. At last half of the referrals made to Graham as the Third Surveyor are now on this subject alone. Sometimes, he has been able to determine that the claimed fees are reasonable. Sadly, however, many of the cases have shown that surveyors are simply charging too much.

Then there is the small works question, which is covered in some detail elsewhere[1]. It is just not fair that the owner of a suburban terraced house, anxious to carry out a small alteration to his property which affects both his neighbours, should have to pay West End fees to three party wall surveyors. The fees very soon begin to wag the works.

A former assistant of John's was once appalled to be told by an Adjoining Owner's Surveyor, working for a well known and formerly respected firm, that his fee would be a minimum of £1,000 (or thereabouts) for a job, the details of which he knew nothing about. John's assistant protested that while he would be perfectly happy to agree an award with a fee of £2,000 if it was justified, he was not prepared to agree to £1,000 if the proper figure was £500. You may be as disturbed as John was to learn that the initial reaction to this was to say, 'Well that's our minimum, and if you won't pay it we'll send the papers back'. Happily, backed by John's enthusiastic endorsement, the assistant succeeded in making the other side see reason.

[1] See Chapter 1.

Of course it costs as much (if not more) for a surveyor to travel from his office to a distant residential job as it does to stroll round to a big commercial development. However, you must temper the wind to the shorn lamb: take a loss on a job, regard it as useful experience, and help the little man to a swift and efficient end to his works. You may even be laying up for yourself treasure in Heaven.

Going to the
Third Surveyor

Suppose you cannot agree upon the basic terms of an award. It doesn't happen very often, but it's not unknown. Suppose you can't agree the Adjoining Owner's Surveyor's fee. This often happens, but is usually compromised. Suppose you can't agree about damage and remedial works. This happens quite frequently. Do you go to law about it? Certainly not. Do you yell and scream abuse at each other? Well, perhaps (depending on your temperament), but it won't get you anywhere. Do you go to the Third Surveyor? You certainly should, and with less diffidence than is often shown. There is nothing to be ashamed about in asking a respected fellow professional to settle an honest difference of opinion, and you should surely have no hesitation in asking the same chap to tell some pig-headed opponent just where he's going wrong.

It is a sad fact that sometimes even surveyors can't agree what it is they disagree upon. This makes it very difficult for the Third Surveyor, as you can imagine. Before approaching the Third Surveyor therefore, make sure you both know what it is you are asking of him. A joint letter from both surveyors setting out the matters in dispute helps to concentrate minds.

Even this does not always work. Graham once had a matter referred to him as the Third Surveyor, in which the Building Owner wanted to underpin next door. The Adjoining Owner's Surveyor claimed that this was not the most appropriate way to safeguard his owner's building, and the dispute came Graham's way.

So that it was clear to everyone, he confirmed to the surveyors that they were asking him to determine whether or not next door's building should be underpinned. Both surveyors confirmed that this was the point at issue.

Graham then made his award, which stated that the adjoining building should be underpinned. Within hours of publishing, the Adjoining Owner's Surveyor was on the telephone screaming, 'Why did you deal with something which we had agreed? I accepted that the wall should be underpinned, but it was the method I disagreed with'. Graham (forbearing to scream, of course) reminded him that he had written confirming what Graham had been asked to deal with. The man duly apologised and said goodbye – but Graham never did find out what he told his owner: probably that the Third Surveyor had made a mistake but that it wasn't worth appealing his award.

Before you refer a dispute to the Third Surveyor comes one of those rare moments when you actually consult your Appointing Owner. The reason for this is that he may be called upon to bear the costs of the reference, and he will definitely be forced to put up with the delay while the matter is decided – as to which, more later. He may well, therefore, decide to submit to some imposition – a restriction on working hours, an inordinate fee – rather than risk the other consequences. Too often, surveyors refer an issue to the Third Surveyor without

95

informing their owner. This is not to say that the surveyor needs an instruction to go to the Third Surveyor, but it is pragmatic to ensure that the owners are aware of the reasons for the referral and the consequences of it.

Discuss the issue of costs between you. Some Adjoining Owners' Surveyors think that all fees, even those of the Third Surveyor, are paid for by the Building Owner regardless – but this is wrong. Often, if an Adjoining Owner thinks there is a possibility he may be picking up a bill, he is less inclined to have the matter determined by another surveyor.

Once your owner, knowing the issues, decides to proceed, you write to your chosen arbiter. You have been told elsewhere[1] that he may not want to have heard of his selection heretofore, and this will therefore probably be the first he knows of the matter. Your first letter should acquaint him very briefly and simply with the outlines of the dispute, and ask him if he is willing to act. It may be helpful to send him at this stage evidence of both surveyors' selection of him, whether in a semi-official form or else simply by an exchange of letters. A signed award, if the disagreement comes after the award, is usually good evidence, as it will probably record his selection.

From here on, the procedure rather depends on the man chosen. However, a typical case might go as follows. On receipt of your letter, the Third Surveyor asks both surveyors to supply evidence of their appointment, copies of notices, and any documents so far agreed. He then

[1] See Chapter 1.

calls both surveyors before him and tries to get at the root of their disagreement. Sometimes this will be all that is needed, and the intervention of a clear-headed outsider will either result in a compromise, or else reveal to one party where he is wrong. This often produces no fee for the Third Surveyor, but enhances his reputation and probably makes him feel good inside.

More often, a problem which is not immediately soluble presents itself. Having heard the first thoughts of the two contestants, the arbitrator/umpire/Third Surveyor (for he is certainly one of those, probably two, and maybe all three) will want to see the scene of the crime. He will arrange access, with both or neither of the two, not with just one of them, and will ask each of them to submit a formal statement of his case, giving the other a copy and an opportunity to comment. It is important that justice should be seen to be done, but it can be dangerous to allow comments on the comments, and comments on those. Things can get out of hand – with, in some cases, neither party able to let a single letter go by without a counterblast from the other. Some follow the practice of requiring both surveyors to submit their case in full to the Third Surveyor, copy to each other, and then allowing each of them one riposte. However, this does put the more prompt man at a disadvantage, because his opponent will have received the case and drafted his original submission accordingly. He will then have waited for the opponent's riposte and replied to that. It is therefore more sensible – in such fraught situations – to have each side send two copies of their submission to the Third Surveyor, and only when he has them both, for him to send the copies out to the other side. The same is done with the ripostes and, if absolutely forced to allow them, the counter-ripostes.

The LBA used to allow the Third Surveyor 14 days to make his award, but very few were held to this. General informed opinion had it that it must mean 14 days after the Third Surveyor was in possession of all the evidence he needed: after all, it frequently takes that length of time for a busy arbiter – and they're likely to be the best sort – to fit in a visit to the site. Recognising the impossibility of laying down a timetable for the Third Surveyor, especially when delays are usually caused by the failure of the other two surveyors to make their submissions quickly, the 1996 Act does not specify when the award must be made: merely that the Third Surveyor must get on and make it. When he has written it out, usually with the same sort of preambles as the customary two-man form, he informs the two surveyors of the fact that it is ready and may be taken up on payment of his fee. He tells them what the total is, and it is then up to them and their owners whether they each pay half of it, or one of them pays the whole.

Within the award itself, probably as the very last clause, will be the directions as to eventual responsibility for the Third Surveyor's fees. Quite often one party will be held liable to pay all the fees – it may well not be that one who was so anxious to collect the award that he quickly paid in full – and sometimes the fees may be split equally or unequally between Building Owner and Adjoining Owner. There is a tendency to regard all disputes as the Building Owner's fault, but one must guard against always making him pay.

When he has received his total fees, the Third Surveyor releases his award and, regardless of who paid, sends it out either to the parties or their surveyors, who must forthwith send the originals on to their Appointing

Owners in accordance with section 10(14). The surveyors might add useful comments on the Third Surveyor's award, including the possibility of appeal if they think that the award is clearly wrong (rather than that it just disagrees with their opinion).

* * *

How should you, a young, inexperienced surveyor, who has refused to be browbeaten by your older opposite number, who tells you that he's done more awards than you've had hot dinners, present your case to the Third Surveyor? First of all, remember that you probably agreed to his selection (unless early argument forced reference to the Appointing Officer[1] even for this element of the equation), so he's not necessarily a potential opponent, nor an ogre. If you've chosen well, your youth will certainly not be held against you – provided that you don't come in chewing gum with a baseball cap turned backwards, and as long as you call him 'sir'.

Don't weary the Third Surveyor with irrelevant history. Stick to the points at issue, and try to keep any personal animosity (and there are lots of good stories on that point) out of your remarks and behaviour. Observe the same strictures in the written presentation of your case. Make sure that all the items in dispute are dealt with: the Third Surveyor won't be pleased to be asked to make a further award because you forgot something. Keep your comments on the other side's representations brief, and make sure that they're clearly related to the originals, using his numbering of paragraphs, if there was any, or making apparent by the use of words what exactly it is that you're rebutting.

---

[1] See Chapter 1.

Do keep comments on the issues in dispute relevant to those issues. Do not make personal comments about the other surveyor, however useless you may think he is. The experienced Third Surveyor will find out for himself if this is true, but to trade insults in correspondence does nothing to assist the process, increases the time everyone has to spend on the matter and puts you in a bad light.

Politely direct the Third Surveyor's attention to any legal matters which you think may assist your case: leading decisions; the wording of certain sections of the Act; this book? Don't regard losing a dispute, or even not wholly winning, as being a slight on your professional reputation. It may be, of course, but in that case all the reading in the world isn't going to help you, because to lose in that way will show that you're not fit to do the job in the first place. Happily, that sort of person is not likely to be reading this book. An honest loss can be an education, or just one more weight in the scale of experience. Do try to win, though, or you shouldn't be there.

Access to next door

Many people think that you have a right to go onto someone else's land to get at your own building. Objections to planning applications are sometimes even made along the lines that this 'right' will be denied the complainant: 'If permission is granted I will be unable to paint my windows/render my wall/clean my gutters!' In 1992 an Act of Parliament granting such a right was indeed passed – the *Access To Neighbouring Land Act 1992*. (For a full exposition of that Act, see the College of Estate Management's study pack of that name, written by John himself, and available from RICS Books.)

The 1992 Act deals only with works to your own building for which you need to go onto a neighbour's land. Moreover, it only covers repairs ('maintenance or preservation'), and not redevelopment. More to the point, it has nothing whatsoever to do with party walls – if you need access to next door for anything to do with them, it's the 1996 Act you should be concerned about, not the 1992 Act.

(Of course, you can still acquire all sorts of rights to go on to other people's land, and even to pick their cabbages, by prescription or grant. Outside these rare occurrences, however, your neighbour's land is his own, even if you try to do work without setting foot on his actual soil, suspended from sky hooks, as *cuius est solus eius est usque ad coelos et ad inferos* which, being translated, means that if he owns the ground then he owns everything from the centre of the earth up to the heavens, always barring government intervention in the matter of minerals, overflying, et cetera. But that is by-the-by for the purposes of this book.)

Under the *Party Wall Act*, you have a very significant right to go onto your neighbour's land. Let us first of all explain what the Act says, and then point out some of the snags.

Section 8(1) says that 'A building owner...may during usual working hours enter...any premises...for executing any work in pursuance of this Act...', which looks fairly straightforward. If you are doing any work under an award[1], because there has been a difference between the owners which has been settled by the surveyors, then quite obviously your rights are clear. If the award envisages your need to go next door to erect scaffolding, or to excavate, or to take down the wall, or to shutter off some part of the Adjoining Owner's building, then section 8 gives you clear power to do so. Furthermore, it goes on to say at 8(2) that you may break down the door with a policeman. (This rather graphic version of this sub-section, which now has quite wide currency, was John's originally and he was very proud of it.) You have to give 14 days notice of your intention, or as much as possible in an emergency.

The involvement of a policeman should really only be as a last resort, if for no other reason than that the

[1] See Chapter 6.

constabulary have enough on their plates without worrying about difficult neighbours. However, standing on the doorstep of next-door's property with a boy in blue can serve to bring an awkward Adjoining Owner to his senses very quickly!

It may occur to some of you that there are times when it is an advantage to have a party wall instead of one of your own. If you want to go next door to do the work, which gives you the better chance, nay, the right? Quite correct: the former. So as long as there's no overriding reason why you need total control of the wall, if next door want to treat it as a party wall, why not let them? In fact, it's an even better bet (although *Marchant v Capital and Counties*[1] may now have changed this), because awards do not run with the land, and so no decision by two surveyors to treat a wall as a party wall (or not, for that matter) can be binding on any surveyors that follow them. Therefore, when it suits a later surveyor to argue that a wall is not party, he can do so. Remember, ownership of the wall is a matter of title, and surveyors are not empowered to decide ownership or boundaries by their position under the Act, if these questions are seriously disputed between the owners. In practice, the surveyors are usually deciding, from the evidence, which category walls come into, and on whose land they are standing, and there is generally no argument. If they deliberately make a wrong decision, it will not be legal, and would be readily appealed against by either owner. None of this is to be taken as encouragement deliberately to argue either way as it suits, but only to point out that if both sides are happy to treat a wall in a certain way, argument may be unnecessary.

[1] See Chapter 16.

Two difficulties in the operation of section 8 can be easily
seen. If you are carrying out work which does not require
an award, under section 1, for example, or even by
express consent to a section 3 notice, it may come as a
considerable shock to the Adjoining Owner to receive
your 14 days' notice of intent to enter, and he may make
some difficulty about it. However, the words are clear:
the Building Owner 'may...enter...any premises...for
executing any work in pursuance of this Act'. It doesn't
even say that it has to be necessary – not at this point –
and it might be argued that in some cases mere
convenience would justify doing the work from the
Adjoining Owner's side. It is to be hoped that responsible
surveyors would not make an award allowing
unnecessary access causing unreasonable inconvenience,
but the permission is certainly very wide. It gets a little
narrower in the last few words of sub-section (1) of
section 8, where the word 'necessary' does appear, and
this is where the second difficulty comes in.

The Building Owner may 'take any other action
necessary for that purpose'. 'Any other action' is so
broad in its scope that 'necessary' only narrows it down
a little. Take a not altogether hypothetical case. A party
wall, agreed to be such because it stands on a boundary
of ownership, doubles as a retaining wall for an uphill
garden, and the external wall of a downhill building.
Either owner has an absolute right to take it down and
rebuild it, but whichever of them does so is going to
cause an awful lot of disturbance to his neighbour,
while it is hardly thinkable that the work can be carried
out without going on to the land of the Adjoining
Owner. If the uphill garden is subsiding, the owner can
only maintain the support by going downhill and
rebuilding, so he must be allowed into the next-door

building. If the downhill property owner wants to rebuild, he may find great difficulty in doing so if he cannot go into next-door's garden and cut back some of the soil while he excavates the old wall and constructs the new.

Either of the parties to such an arrangement is going to be unhappy when whichever happens to be the Building Owner tells the other of his plans, and they will probably argue at length as to whether what the Building Owner proposes is lawful. When forced to concede the existence of section 8, the Adjoining Owner will rely on 'necessary', and demand that the Building Owner prove his necessity. When all three surveyors have adjudicated on the subject, one party may well appeal the award of the Third Surveyor.

Let us consider an even more straightforward – or is it? – case. As you have read[1], under section 1(5) a Building Owner may build a wall on his own land at the line of junction without objection from the Adjoining Owner, but must serve notice of his intention. As there is no provision for objection, there can be no appointment of surveyors and no award. He can just get on with it, including putting foundations on next-door's land. Now, as we noted a few paragraphs above, section 8 says nothing about work under an award, or appointment of surveyors. It simply says that 'A building owner…may…enter…and may execute any work in pursuance of this Act'. Well, section 1(5) is in 'this Act', so it seems that the Building Owner is entitled to the benefit of section 8. But must he go on to next-door's land to do the construction works?

[1] In Chapter 3.

Certainly it will be easier for him if he can scaffold the building externally, and get on with other jobs inside, not to mention the fact that the wall will look so much nicer. Actually, it pays to mention this fact to next door, even if outside the Act, because it is they who will be looking at the wall after it's built, and they should prefer to see a neater wall. If, however, there was a building next door, built right up to the line of junction, you obviously couldn't go into it in order to erect a fair-faced wall, nor would you want to, as nobody would be going to see its face, fair or otherwise. Therefore, is it necessary to go on to the Adjoining Owner's land if there is no building there?

The authors' opinion is that the necessity must be a matter of judgment for the surveyors. It is also arguable that section 10 covers the settlement of any argument between the owners. Remember that the section starts by saying: 'Where a dispute arises...'. 'Dispute' is not a term of art, and does not mean only a formal dissent under section 1, 3 or 6. The clause goes on to say 'in respect of any matter connected with any work to which this Act relates', so that if a Building Owner served notice of entry under section 8, for whatever purpose, and an Adjoining Owner disputed it, their difference should be settled under section 10[1].

These issues can be difficult, and have taken a while to be resolved by legislation. Hopefully, though, this chapter has managed to shed some light on the matters.

---

[1] See Chapter 1.

Who pays for what?

It is a common fallacy that the Building Owner is bound by the Act to pay the Adjoining Owner's Surveyor's fees. The Act makes no such categorical statement. At section 10(13) it says that the reasonable costs of 'making or obtaining an award', together with the cost of reasonable supervision of the works, shall be paid according to the award of the surveyors. In fact, this means that in 99 cases out of 100, the Building Owner does pay, but only because that is what the surveyors decide.

It is of course reasonable that any costs directly arising from the Building Owner's intention to build should fall upon him, and therefore the reasonable fees of the surveyor necessarily appointed by the Adjoining Owner, both to prepare the award and to keep an eye on the property while the works are being carried out, should form a natural extension of those costs. However, some argument has arisen as to what is a necessary part of 'making or obtaining' that award. Quite apart from discussion as to the reasonableness of fees in general,[1] there are frequent disagreements over the incidence of solicitors' fees and those of consulting engineers.

[1] See Chapter 7.

Solicitors' fees are easily dealt with. There is no need for a solicitor anywhere in the proper operation of the Act, and therefore just because an Adjoining Owner, on receiving a notice, has consulted his solicitor, there is no justification for charging his fees to the Building Owner. However, if the Building Owner has attempted to proceed without due regard for the procedural niceties, so that the services of a solicitor have been necessary to get him to go through the proper motions, then it would seem fair to argue that the fees for those services have been properly incurred in 'obtaining' an award, and the surveyors should not hesitate to award their payment.

Engineers' fees are a little more tricky – and a little more frequently paid – but in essence they follow the same principle. If the Adjoining Owner's Surveyor has called in an engineer to advise whether the bricks should be red or yellow, or whether the underpinning should be done in bays of three feet or one metre, then the engineer's fees should not fall on the Building Owner. However, if the works are of such complexity that they fall outside the competence of a reasonably able building surveyor, then those making the award are likely to agree that a consultant's fees are a necessary charge. The above makes it clear why it is beholden upon anyone undertaking work as a party wall surveyor[1] to make sure that he is competent to deal with the technical matters involved. If he is not, he should refuse the appointment. Alas for vanity, this good advice is not heeded often enough in more fields than party wall surveying but, oh joy!, how much work comes thereby to expert witnesses.

There are certain direct instructions as to responsibility for costs of construction in what one might call the prime

---

[1] And see Chapter 1 for the necessary qualifications.

moving sections of the 1996 Act: 1, 2, and 6. In 1(3)(b) the cryptic remark is made that the cost of building a new party wall or party fence wall 'shall be from time to time defrayed by the two owners in such proportion as has regard to the use made or to be made of the wall by…' and goes on to add that such defraying shall also respect 'the cost of labour and materials prevailing at the time when that use is made…'. This becomes less cryptic when read in conjunction with 11(11) and 11 (7)[1]. It covers situations such as where Mr Black, who is building a wall, needs a four-storey warehouse wall[2], while all Mr Blue (on the other side) needs is a garden wall. Mr Blue therefore pays half the cost of the garden wall. If, later, Mr Blue wants to use more than a two-metre-high garden wall, he can be called upon to pay a fair, current market, contribution.

Section 2 is a little more subtle in handing out responsibility, which is why you should always carefully observe which sub-section is quoted in a notice. The main difference is between 2(2)(a) and (b) or (e), as you will see when you reach the discussion of section 11 which follows in a page or so.

Under section 6, meanwhile, there is a plain direction that the Building Owner is responsible for the cost of any necessary underpinning (or strengthening or safeguarding) of the Adjoining Owner's foundations.

It goes without saying that the Building Owner is responsible for any damage that is caused by the works carried out under the award, but that responsibility is rather more firmly fixed under the Act than it is under

---

[1] See later in this chapter.
[2] The astute may notice a subtle reference to a real case.

common law. Not only is the Building Owner made directly and specifically liable for any damage caused under certain sections, to which we shall very shortly come, but also the award firmly states, in almost every case, that he shall immediately make good any damage occasioned to the structure or decorations of the Adjoining Owner's premises – or words to that effect. The Adjoining Owner cannot then be fobbed off by being referred to the management contractor, to the main contractor, to the sub-contractor, to the sub-contractor's insurers, or to the insurer's loss adjusters. That now only happens to the Building Owner's Surveyor, who finds himself pursued by all those people for having prejudiced their position by agreeing a figure of damages with the Adjoining Owner's Surveyor. Bully for him. He has acted in accordance with the law and the award, and he has settled the matter in dispute between the owners. How the Building Owner settles it on his side and where he fixes the ultimate responsibility is up to him, but the man who has suffered has been properly and promptly indemnified.

An award is not, however, a let-out for a Building Owner if the Adjoining Owner's Surveyor has approved a method of working which then proves to be inadequate to protect his Appointing Owner. The case of *Brace v South-East Regional Housing Association*[1], although not a *London Building Act* case, makes this clear, as does section 6(10) of the 1996 Act. The Building Owner is always responsible for the results of his actions, although as we saw in Chapter 3, this could give rise to injustice if he is not allowed to take the precautions which he thinks desirable.

[1] See Chapter 16 for further discussion of this case.

As it is apparent that almost any party wall work is likely to risk causing damage, it is curious that the Act singles out certain operations for which the Building Owner is specifically liable. No doubt some day someone really intent on a legal battle will claim that inclusion of some sub-sections must be deemed to exclude all others, but surveyors are generally more sensible. It is worth noting, however, just which sub-sections do include an express liability, and they are: 1(7); 2(2)(a) (e) (f) (g) (h) and (j); and 7(2).

The first time that compensation is mentioned is in section 1(7), where any damage from placing footings on the land of an Adjoining Owner is to be made good to that owner and any occupier. Such cases are very rare (although gardeners have been known to wax wrathful if their flower beds are not reinstated). Then comes section 2, and while you can carry out fantastic acts of demolition and rebuilding under sub-sections (b) to (d) without causing any damage apparently (possibly because the works are for the joint benefit of Building and Adjoining Owners), when you get to (e) you are liable to cause the damage and to pay for it, and so on, until you reach (j). However, you can then do (k) (l) (m) and (n) without penalty. You can find these sub-sections elsewhere[1], so they won't be repeated here, but it does seem strange that the Act does not say simply: any damage to the adjoining premises shall be made good at the cost of whichever party the surveyors shall decide. There is a kind of logic to who's in, who's out, but as some of the outs are likely to have to come in, it all seems rather pointless.

---

[1] See Chapter 3.

Anstey's Party Walls

You may be surprised to hear that there is no specific liability for repair should you have cause to break down the door with a policeman (section 8)[1].

There is a whole section of the Act, section 11, devoted simply to 'Expenses', which deals with the payment for actual building works. It is quite logical and simply summed up: if the work is for the sole benefit of the Building Owner, then he pays, but if the Adjoining Owner derives some benefit, then he contributes his fair share.

Sub-section (1) says that the Building Owner always pays, except where the rest of the section says otherwise. If the work is of repair to the party wall, the expense is apportioned according to the use made of the wall and the responsibility for the defect.

The provisions of 11(7) are a little more complicated. If the Building Owner seeks to reduce the height of an existing wall (under 2(2)(m)), the Adjoining Owner can require him to keep it up by paying an appropriate share of the modern cost of its construction.

We can look at section 11(6) in conjunction with section 2(2)(e) – the big one. That's when the whole party wall may be pulled down, leaving you exposed to the cold night air[2]. You certainly will have suffered inconvenience as you are shuttered off from the party wall, and then rejoined to it. You will have been deprived of the use of a certain amount of space for a certain period, which should be fairly easy to value, and you will also have

---

[1] See Chapter 9.
[2] Or, more probably, other measures adopted: see Chapter 3.

been inconvenienced in a more general way: cramped, dirty, workmen in and out. Section 11(6) says that the Adjoining Owner is to be paid a 'fair allowance in respect of disturbance and inconvenience'. If only it were possible to offer concrete guidance on how to assess such disturbance. We can only suggest that it may be helpful to agree the easily established costs as quickly as possible and then, perhaps, agree a percentage addition to reflect the less easily assessable losses.

Frankly, there is no way that springs to mind to make these provisions exciting to read about. They are hardly ever brought into discussion, as they mostly state the obvious. As this is meant to be a comprehensive work, we should continue ploughing on, but if you're not already asleep, why not save this bit of the book until you want a nap.

Sub-section (9) says that if the Adjoining Owner demands that the Building Owner has to carry out some additional works, then he has to pay for what he asked for. That's reasonable isn't it? Similarly reasonable is sub-section (10), which makes the Building Owner refund to the Adjoining Owner any additional costs to which the latter is later put because of the existence of reinforced foundations. A warning is not entirely out of place here with regard to using special foundations. Briefly, it is a bad idea to have special foundations, even if next door readily consents. When the difficulties of dealing with them and the additional costs thereof actually arise, neither owner on either side of the party wall may even be aware of their existence. The present Building Owner, who sees his programme set back some considerable time by the reinforcing, will not be happy, and nor will the current Adjoining Owner (erstwhile Building Owner's successor) when he receives – out of the blue – a bill for the extra costs. So don't do it.

Finally, we come to sub-section (11) itself, which simply says that when an Adjoining Owner later makes use of work paid for by the former Building Owner, he has to pay the appropriate share of the current cost of that work.

In case it's not obvious how this situation arises, let's take an example. Two semi-detached houses stand side by side (obviously). The owner of the left-hand property puts in a loft extension, raising the party wall to enclose it and he pays all the cost. Ten years later, his neighbour in the right-hand house decides that he would like a loft extension. He has a right to use the already raised wall, as it is party, but he has to pay his share of the modern cost of construction. Almost certainly, the recipient of the payment will be the current freeholder of next door.

Sub-section (11) also says that payment must be in current money values. In other words, when the Building Owner discovers that it's going to cost him £2,000 to enclose on next-door's wall, it's no good saying that it would only have cost the (now) Adjoining Owner £500 five years ago. The sum to be refunded is the present cost. The same must be true of other payments, for example, for extra costs caused by special foundations under 11(10). One way out of this is to agree the cost of doing the work at that point, and for the then Building Owner to pay it to the then Adjoining Owner. The latter can do what he wants with it: he can buy the entire recorded oeuvre of Bix Beiderbecke; or he can invest it and realise it when he comes to do his own work. The Adjoining Owner should have no objection to this way of dealing with the matter, but he cannot compel the Building Owner to do it: the latter can quite properly refrain from paying until the work is about to be done. You may be confused about who is the Building Owner and who is the Adjoining Owner. The answer is that, in these questions, they have swapped sides, and you can probably call each of them either.

Who, by the way, is the Building Owner from whom this sum is to be recovered? Is he the chap who did the work (and where is he now?) or the present freeholder or the tenant on a full repairing lease? Sue someone, and you might find out the answer: in the authors' opinion, it's the current freeholder.

'Security for expenses' is provided for in section 12 of the Act. It operates in two directions: first, if the Adjoining Owner fears that the Building Owner's operations may leave him unstable (financially or structurally), he can ask the Building Owner to put up a sum of money (this is quite often done when the latter only has an address abroad); second, if the Adjoining Owner requires the Building Owner to carry out work for which the former may have to pay all or part of the cost, the latter may ask for security. Security could be necessary for those things which might put an Adjoining Owner to expense if the Building Owner fails to honour his obligations, such as removing scaffolding, providing permanent weathering to an exposed party wall, installing permanent restraint and removing the temporary support, and so on. After all, is it fair an Adjoining Owner should be left out of pocket because of a Building Owner's failure to meet his responsibilities?

That does not mean that you should always request security against possible damage, but undoubtedly the

115

fear of damage prompts a large proportion of the requests for security which are made.

The provisions of security under section 12(1) are very wide ranging. Look at the section:

> 'An Adjoining Owner may serve a notice requiring the Building Owner before he begins any work in the exercise of the rights conferred by this Act to give such security as may be agreed between the owners or in the event of dispute determined in accordance with Section 10.'

It is only when the owners cannot agree upon whether security should be provided, or the amount, that the appointed surveyors deal with the issue under section 10. In these instances, the surveyors should make an award confirming their opinion.

As most owners will not be aware of the provisions of section 12, surveyors should guide them on the matter. Again, to repeat, this is not to say that every job justifies security. Common sense must prevail. In a residential situation, a request for security from an Adjoining Owner can create ill-feeling with the Building Owner. In effect, the Adjoining Owner is saying, 'I don't trust you to do what you say you are going to do'. So even though the Adjoining Owner is entitled to ask for security, there are practical implications in doing so, and you should ensure that the Appointing Owner is aware of them.

Graham was once involved in a case in which it was proposed to demolish a building and leave the party wall exposed, with temporary weatherproofing and restraint. The other side could not guarantee when – or indeed, if –

it would start rebuilding. Graham therefore asked for security for expenses, to begin if the other side had not commenced rebuilding after 12 months. Despite their protestations and injured feelings, three years later, rebuilding had yet to begin. The sum for security in this case was a quarter of a million pounds – in a small residential case, it could be as low as several hundred pounds.

Fortunately, whereas under the LBA the only method of settling arguments about security for expenses was through the courts, the new Act gives all the procedures of section 10, that is to say the three surveyors, for use in the first instance, with the County Court available for an appeal if the parties are not content to accept the surveyors' determination.

This is one (or two, depending on how you look at it) of the reasons why changes of ownership during the progress of works, or during the period of notice, may make it necessary either for the proceedings to begin *de novo*, or for the parties to be bound by what has gone before (for a detailed discussion of this point, see Chapter 11).

Note that it is the owners who have to ask for security, not the surveyors – even though the surveyors are more likely to know whether security is needed, as they will not only be aware of the structural risks which may be being taken, but may also have met the particular developer before and know, for example, that it will prove difficult to extract reparation if things do go wrong.

We may be sure, however, that the surveyors will be well to the fore in the background to start with, and possibly later even in the foreground, because the most common way of dealing with security money is to put it on deposit in the name of the appropriate party, usually the Building Owner, and provide that it shall only be disbursed on the instructions of any two of the three surveyors. In many cases, nothing is required to be paid out and the whole sum, together with accumulated interest, is returned to the original depositor. Arguments have been advanced that the interest should be shared, but they can be rejected, as the non-depositor has no right to anything save his security, and if he has needed no indemnification, then all the money reverts to its provider.

Finally, if you're still awake, or if the exciting provisions of sections 11 and 12 have re-awoken you, we come to section 13. Extraordinarily, the surveyors now step back into action. Section 13 requires the Building Owner to submit a formal account for any work to which the Adjoining Owner is required to contribute, within two months of completion of the works in question, and says that if the owners disagree about any rates, apportionment or other like matters, 'a dispute shall be deemed to have arisen' – and we all know who settles disputes.

The effective last section of all (because there are still some technical sections to come[1]) is not the most exciting. It merely states that until the Adjoining Owner has paid up his share, the Building Owner retains sole ownership of the works in question. Hooray for him, though what good it does him is hard to understand.

---

[1] See Chapters 5 and 13.

Change of ownership

This is one of those matters on which there is not really any useful legal guidance – and the authors have therefore had to work out their own ideas on the points in issue.

If the Building Owner changes during the course of works, before or after an award has been drawn up, then the whole proceedings have to start *de novo*. The Act is very personal in its application, and there is no obvious authority therein for the transfer of rights by a vendor Building Owner to his successor in title. When drawing up an award, the two surveyors may be influenced in the way clauses are worded by their personal knowledge – or lack of it – of the track record of the developers: whether they always honour their obligations under an award and (which is not always so easy) whether they see that the contractors do; whether the Adjoining Owner's Surveyors' fees are promptly paid; whether damage is quickly put right or paid for; whether noisy works are carefully controlled. All these factors may influence the rigidity of an award. Furthermore, the whole emphasis of the Act is a personal one: you do not appoint a firm, you appoint a surveyor[1]; an award does not bind land or sites, it binds owners. In conclusion, therefore, you

[1] See Chapter 1.

cannot pass the benefit of an award to an incoming owner. He may be quite unknown to the Adjoining Owner and his surveyor or, often worse, well known.

If you consider the question of security for expenses[1] under section 12, you will realise that an Adjoining Owner may readily allow a particular Building Owner to start work, even of a sort which puts the former's building at considerable risk, without asking for any security, relying upon the latter's reputation for fair dealing and financial soundness, whereas if the property is disposed of to a man (or company) of altogether less exalted reputation, the Adjoining Owner may want very ample security indeed. It would therefore surely be inequitable that the benefits of section 12 should be denied him: the negotiations must start afresh with the service of new notice in the new name. However, the Building Owner who served the original notice cannot escape the consequences of that service by disposing of the property. Any damage done or fees incurred will be his liability, although very often the kindly purchaser will relieve him of it. *Selby v Whitbread*[2] is a case that bears on this point.

There is also the problem of the change of ownership that has been known about and anticipated all along, to which we alluded when dealing with the service of the notice[3]. An intending purchaser is to be the developer, and wants to get everything in order and prepared for starting before he completes his purchase, but until he has a contract to purchase he does not (it seems) come within

[1] See Chapter 10.
[2] See Chapter 16.
[3] See Chapter 5.

the Act's definition of an owner. It is hard on him if he has to wait two months after contract, when all the details could have been tied up in an award long before. A possible solution is for both parties, vendor and purchaser, to join in service of the notice. The legality of this procedure might be slightly dubious, but it is certainly an equitable procedure, as Adjoining Owners know from the outset who they are really going to be dealing with, and yet notice is served, albeit jointly, well in advance by the then owner of the legal interest.

This system and theory could be extended to deal – at least partly – with the purchaser who buys during the progress of a job. As soon as the vendor knows that he has the deal as good as concluded, he could serve new notices in the joint names of himself and the purchaser, so that the new negotiations could be got on with and the new awards produced while the writ of the old awards continued to run. On completion, the new awards would supersede the old, with no awkward hiatus. Of course, in most cases additional fees would be incurred, but in comparison with the cost of delay, they'd be cheap at the price. However, it must be pointed out that not everyone agrees with this theory. The alternative solution is to serve in the present owner's name, proceed as far as possible and, when the new owner is properly entitled so to be called, serve fresh notices and beg the Adjoining Owners to waive the period of notice.

The position of an Adjoining Owner who disposes of or acquires an interest is more complicated and yet perhaps more obvious. It is obviously inequitable for a Building Owner who has done everything properly to be frustrated by the sale of an Adjoining Owner's property. (The more alert among you will have noticed this emphasis on the question of equity: that is because the authors believe this is the approach the courts would take, in the absence of express legislation on the point.) An Adjoining Owner who was absolutely determined to thwart or, at the very least, postpone for as long as possible the intended works of a Building Owner, could move the property around between subsidiary companies or friends and relations, forcing the service of fresh notices every time, if that were a legal manoeuvre.

But that cannot be right. The Act gives a Building Owner certain rights, and it must be intended that, provided he fulfils his duties properly, he should not be improperly impeded in the exercise of them.

What, then, is the position of an Adjoining Ownership which changes its identity? In the opinion of the authors, a vendor or lessor is bound fully to disclose to any purchaser or lessee the existence of party wall negotiations and the extent to which they have proceeded. The latter will be bound by those proceedings, as far as they have gone to date. If notice has been served, the new Adjoining Owner needs no new notice. If a surveyor has been appointed, that surveyor must carry on acting for the new owner. If an award has been made, then the incoming owner is bound by that award just as much as if he had been the person on whom notice was originally served. The authors would argue that these guidelines apply equally whether an interest is disposed of from (say) one freeholder to another, or whether a subsidiary interest is created from (say) a head-lessee to a sub-lessee.

In fact, there should be no serious difficulties on this side of the wall, as it is hard to believe that a sale or lease could be completed more quickly than a party wall award, provided that the surveyors knew that there was some urgency about the matter. All it needs is for anyone who is thinking of getting rid of their holding to tell their appointed surveyor – it will all be much tidier if the award is in existence and the new owner takes possession with full knowledge of it.

Unfortunately, in all the excitement of making a financial killing in the disposal, the owner frequently forgets to tell his appointed surveyor at all – or his successor in title. The first that either party knows about it is when the surveyor pops in to see how things are going, and sees a strange face, while the strange face wonders who this is barging in as if he owns the place. This innocent purchaser might perhaps have a right of action against the vendor, if he felt that he had not bought what he bargained for, but nevertheless, he is firmly fettered by the proceedings already under way.

Some words of advice on this subject. When the Adjoining Owner changes during the course of the works, it is an enormous benefit if the Adjoining Owner's Surveyor explains the procedures to the new owner, spelling out what has arisen to date and what is going to happen when the works are finished. This does two things: it helps to put the mind of a concerned Adjoining Owner at rest, and secondly, shows the Adjoining Owner that the surveyor knows what he is talking about. The Adjoining Owner is more likely to accept that the award still applies, as does the appointment of his surveyor. While not crucial, for the avoidance of doubt, the new Adjoining Owner could then drop his surveyor a line to say that he has no problem with that surveyor continuing to act.

Occasionally, a new Adjoining Owner wants to appoint his own surveyor. This should be discouraged – the present surveyor should stand firm. However, if diplomatic incapacity befalls the surveyor (and this does sometimes happen), the Adjoining Owner should be warned that the fees of his new surveyor may not be met, either in part, or full, by the Building Owner.

One little difficulty that actually happened to John concerned the question of who receives any compensation under section 11, and at what moment does the compensation become payable? When the award is signed, or when the additional use is actually made? Suppose the money is paid with the award, but the disposal takes place before the use is made. Should the first owner pay the money over to the second owner? In the actual case in which John was involved, he was in possession of the cheque for the section 11 compensation when the change of ownership took place. Neither party knew about it, as he had negotiated the matter as a natural part of his duties as the Adjoining Owner's Surveyor, and was going to break the glad news to the Adjoining Owner when he signed and delivered the award. At that very moment, John was informed of the sale. His solution was to ask the vendor whether he had conveyed the property with the full benefit and burden of the party wall proceedings to the purchaser. He replied that he had and so, without revealing why he had asked the question, John paid the money over to the delighted new owner.

If it is possible to sum up this chapter, we could do so by saying that when the Building Owner changes, so does everything else, but when the Adjoining Owner changes, everything goes on as if he hadn't. At least, that's the authors' view of it.

12 An appeal

An appeal is a disaster. A reference to the Third Surveyor is not. The reason for this dichotomy is that the latter is subject to implicit time restrictions, whereas the former is not. It can fairly be said that one of the functions of the Act is to keep negotiations between owners proceeding at a reasonable pace, but naturally it stops short of imposing time limits on the courts, and that's where an appeal is dealt with.

Very, very occasionally an appeal is justified by the fact that an award goes beyond the powers of the surveyors: *Gyle-Thompson*[1] was such a case. Then, faced by an award which allows a Building Owner to do something to which he has no right, the Adjoining Owner has no option but to ask the courts to protect him. But the wheels of the law grind very slowly indeed, and the poor Building Owner may find himself unable to get on with his work at all while the matter drags through the inexorable legal processes.

What can be done – on your part – to avoid such an awful fate? First of all, of course, you should try never to go beyond your powers in an award, and to see that both owners' rights are constantly in your mind when drawing

[1] See Chapter 16.

one up. That's at least one good reason for following a reliable model, as recommended elsewhere[1]. You are less likely to go astray if you are on the rails of good guidance than if you are rambling down an unmarked path.

Second, remember that your Appointing Owner has the right to appeal. When publishing the award, inform him of his rights of appeal, explain what the award deals with and draw his attention to those bits which may cause him concern. Explain why things are as they are. Doing this should in fact make it less likely that your owner will appeal. Uninformed owners can be suspicious ones, whose only option when receiving an award they are worried about is to appeal it. This can be avoided with the surveyor taking a little time to converse with them – often just on the telephone.

If you have lost an argument in front of the Third Surveyor, who has agreed with your opposite number, and you think that you were so right that the decision against you is not just unfavourable, but wrong, then no doubt you not only have a duty to *inform* your Appointing Owner of his rights of appeal, but perhaps also to encourage him to exercise these.

Unfortunately, there are those who have what a judge recently described as an exaggerated sense of their rights, and such people can be prepared to appeal against an award simply to cause maximum inconvenience to their neighbour, without worrying too much about whether they are justified in doing so (if their blinkered vision even allows them to take an unbiased view of the situation). Such people should be told that they are

---

[1] See Chapter 6.

bound by the Act and the award, and on no account *encouraged* to appeal.

An award continues to be of full effect, despite the fact that an appeal has been made, and Building Owners may be comforted to know that most authorities are now agreed that you do not have to stop work because of an appeal. What, they ask, is an injunction for? If the Building Owner and/or his surveyor are perfectly confident that an award is in order, and that the appeal is merely a thwarting device, then they could simply call the bluff of their antagonist and keep working. If the Adjoining Owner asks the courts for an interlocutory injunction, he will be at risk for costs if he eventually loses his action. However, while this is a nice thought, the Building Owner (and his surveyor) must be sure of their ground.

A Building Owner may naturally be reluctant to carry on with his work during the appeal process. After all, if the appeal is upheld, he might then have to undo what he has done. Nevertheless, it is sometimes in both parties' interests that work started should be carried through to completion, for example, if underpinning is intended and the excavation has started. This is also true, by the way, if work has started before the proper formalities have been complied with. It may be preferable to complete the immediate job, and then bring matters to a halt while notices are served and awards prepared. Adjoining Owners (it is usually they who appeal, rather than Building Owners) should be persuaded – if possible – to agree to that element of the work proceeding to completion.

Remember that an appeal could easily take a year in the courts, and at the very least is going to hold up progress for some months. We can only repeat that you should aim to avoid any possibility of an appeal, by your impeccable conduct in serving the notices and agreeing the award, and by working hard to discourage an over-zealous owner whose desire to appeal is not matched by the justice of his cause. If there has to be an appeal, then under section 10 (17) your Appointing Owner has only those 14 days already mentioned in which to enter his appeal in the County Court, if he wants to be sure of its being acceptable – although there are no doubt cases where the courts would justify themselves in accepting appeals out of time, on grounds of equity or natural justice.

There is no respondent, as such, in an appeal. John was once cited in an appeal against his Third Surveyor's award, and the judge, in dismissing him from the action, remarked that it was as if *he* was asked to appear before the Court of Appeal to justify *his* decision in a case. Nor, strictly speaking, is the other owner a respondent: a Building Owner may well wish to appear in court to support an award which an Adjoining Owner is trying to have set aside, but his position is not truly analogous with that of a defendant. A reliable legal authority advises, however, that the other party to an award is likely to be treated as the respondent by the courts, and that costs might be awarded against him if he doesn't appear in court. After all, according to this authority, it will be perceived that if the other party doesn't feel strongly enough about the issue to contest it, he could have avoided the costs by agreeing what the appellant sought in the first place. Nevertheless, it seems to be true that you don't have to name anyone in your approach to the courts: the owner simply appeals against the decision of the surveyor or surveyors. But – to speak directly to such owners – please don't, unless absolutely necessary.

13 Penalties

It is not always easy to enforce performance of a party wall award. There is an excellent timetable for ensuring that one is *produced* of course, with methods of dealing with dilatory or obstructive surveyors, but naturally those methods are rarely needed, because you're dealing with surveyors, who are eminently sensible, industrious and co-operative chaps. It's getting the owners and the contractors to behave that's the difficulty. John's father (himself an eminent surveyor) used to say that all builders were rogues: the only difference between them was that some were likeable rogues. He didn't have a generalisation for Building Owners, but if he had, it would probably have referred to their speed of paying their surveyors' fees.

If you meet a real bad hat, who refuses to serve notices, to appoint a surveyor, or anything like that, there is only one solution: to apply for an injunction. There is no doubt that you'll get it, because in *Bennett v Howell* [1] there was only a dot missing off one 'i', more or less, yet Mrs Bennett got her injunction. To some extent, these are the simpler cases. They're clear cut, and an injunction is a familiar remedy which the law will readily enforce.

---

[1] See Chapter 16.

The problem lies more in getting the Building Owner and/or his contractor to put right minor items of damage, or the former to pay fees due to the Adjoining Owner's Surveyor. We've already said that the surveyor should not refuse to sign an award just because he hasn't yet received his fees[1]. If you, as a Building Owner's Surveyor, meet this proper response from your opposite number, it behoves you to do your best to see that your Appointing Owner pays up. Apart from moral pressure, there is one section of the Act which can assist you. It used to dwell among the untrodden ways of Part XII of the LBA, a section which there were none to praise and very few to love[2] (or at any rate use). Indeed it wasn't even the whole section, 148, but a tiny sub-section, (xix). In the new, shorter, Act it is only section 17, and therefore much more likely to be read. Taken together with section 11(8), which allows the Adjoining Owner to ask for money instead of having work carried out, it makes any sum due under the Act (except fines) summarily recoverable as a civil debt.

The LBA used to make failure to pay up or observe an award an offence punishable in the magistrates' court. That sanction is now reserved for refusing to allow entry to an authorised person or obstructing someone from doing works which he is entitled to do, under section 16 of the 1996 Act.

This chapter is perhaps the best place to discuss what to do when you discover that work is well under way, or even complete, without the benefit of any procedures under the Act. As noted above, if you are up against a

[1] See Chapter 6.
[2] Wordsworth, of course.

villain, you'll need an injunction to bring him to heel. However, if your neighbour is merely ignorant, lazy or absent-minded, milder measures may suffice to clear up the situation. There are many surveyors who bemoan the lack of real punishment for those who refuse to conform, and the loss of the former summary procedure is regrettable in many ways, but there is no need for outright despair. There are very few real rascals who persist in carrying on with work once the need for a notice has been pointed out to them, and the injunction will always be there to deal with the absolutely intransigent.

There is certainly no legal basis for retrospective notices or awards, and yet they are arguably the best method for getting procedures belatedly under way. As the alternative option for the Building Owner is to be injuncted, he should have no objection, and as the Adjoining Owner will obtain an award, with a surveyor (paid for) to look after his interests, far cheaper than by going to law, he should be equally happy. This is not of course, expressly legally sanctioned, but on one or two occasions the courts appear to have tacitly approved this method of dealing with party wall matters which have proceeded ahead of their proper formalities.

Easements

Party wall awards have nothing to do with easements. We could end this chapter there, but that would prevent us from plugging other books, especially the forthcoming new edition of *Anstey's Rights of Light – and how to deal with them*[1], and even more especially, if you really want to learn about the subject in depth, *Gale on Easements*[2]. However, it does need a few more words to drive home the obvious (this will be a good chapter to read if you're feeling tired, because it's impossible to spin the subject out for more than a couple of pages).

As section 9 seems to make it quite clear that no award can override an easement, it might seem that the first sentence of this chapter would suffice. However, the fact that RICS has felt it necessary to include a clause in its sample draft award which specifically states that 'nothing in the award shall be held as conferring, admitting or affecting any right to light or air or any other easement whatsoever' does show that the point needs ramming home. A Building Owner should not be left with the impression that because he has an award he can ignore his neighbour's other rights, but in fact, the clause is included more to spell out to an Adjoining Owner, unfamiliar with section 9, that his rights are unaffected.

[1] RICS Books, due in 2005.
[2] Sweet and Maxwell, 17th Edition, 2002.

It is, unfortunately, not only the Adjoining Owner, but also his surveyor, who is all too often ignorant of section 9 – or if he knows about it, refuses to act as if he did. Surveyors frequently decline to get on with awards because 'my client' (it's the sort of surveyor who calls his Appointing Owner his client who most often makes this kind of difficulty) 'is very worried about his light and has told me not to sign an award until that's sorted out'! Point him towards section 9; explain that party walls are statutory and rights of light are common law; explain that the award gives the Building Owner no right to ignore the Adjoining Owner's rights; and tell him that if he doesn't act within ten days, either you'll proceed *ex parte*, or else you will go to the Third Surveyor and ask for an award of fees against his Appointing Owner because his surveyor has made the approach to the Third Surveyor necessary. That should do the trick.

With regard to windows – and in brief – section 9 makes it clear that if you have a window in a party wall, to which you have acquired an easement, you have every right to take down the wall and rebuild it, retaining the window and its rights.

The other area in which one ought perhaps to consider easements, before rejecting them, is in the matter of overhanging eaves and projecting footings. But for the Act, you could obtain easements to retain such features; however, under section 2(2), paragraphs (g) and (h) specifically give the Building Owner the right to cut them off if they get in the way of his building.

Easement law and party wall legislation are different: keep the two things separate.

Some party wall problems

When are two lots of foundations each lower than the other? Who owns a wall you paid to have built? What notice do you serve if you're constructing a lift pit adjacent to a party wall? Do you always have to serve notice if your new foundations are lower than those of the next-door building? What is 'laying open'? Should the named surveyor do it all by himself? Who is exempt from the Act? What qualifies for security for expenses? Can you raise a party wall on a cantilever?

The reason for lumping all these questions together in this chapter, although they may be touched on – even at some length – elsewhere in the book, is because people are not in complete agreement on the answers. In this chapter, we put forward not so much the consensus (if there is one), as our own views on the correct answers, so that hereafter people can say: 'The standard textbook on the subject says...'. That way, we will get agreement and, as Solon said: 'It is better that the law should be certain than that it should be just'.

Question 1: when are two lots of foundations each lower than the other – and when do you serve notice? *Short answer:* when one is piled and the other is on strip foundations (and there is no short answer with regard to notice). *Longer answer:* if you are building a new building on piles, next door to an old building, and within the three metre (or six metre) provisions of section 6, you would naturally serve notice. Later, the older building may be redeveloped on traditional foundations, which go below the pile caps (but not, of course, the piles) of the new building. Many surveyors would again serve notice, to be on the safe side, because in between the pile caps the new strip foundation would, of course, be lower than the bottom of the new adjoining structure. (See diagrams overleaf for a view of this.)

It should be emphasised that there is only one legal answer. The bottom of foundations is the bottom of foundations and the relative depths of pile caps and edge beams have nothing to do with it. Therefore, the new traditional founds are not, in law, below the Adjoining Owner's foundations. In this paradoxical situation, many surveyors will behave as noted above, in order to have a professional acting for the Adjoining Owner, agreeing schedules and sorting out problems. The professional would be well advised, however, not to serve unnecessary notices which are not strictly within the Act, without advising the Building Owner of the circumstances.

Question 2: who owns a wall you paid to have built? *Short answer:* according to *Gyle-Thompson*[1], the person whose land it stands on. *Longer answer:* the reason advanced by Brightman, J. for saying that Walstreet had no right to reduce the height of a party wall was that the wall stood astride the boundary, and therefore each side owned the part of the wall standing on their land. In John's opinion (with which Graham concurs), this was the wrong view. Even under the LBA, it was envisaged

[1] See Chapter 16.

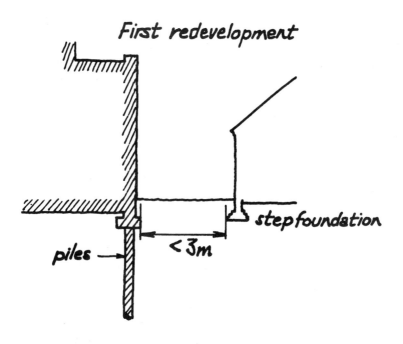

First redevelopment

piles

< 3m

step foundation

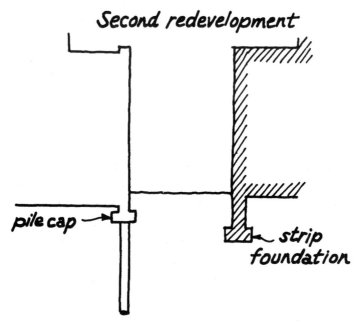

Second redevelopment

pile cap

strip foundation

that an Adjoining Owner was going to have to pay for additional later use. In some people's opinion, that included when requiring the Building Owner to keep up a wall which he had built and paid for. The 1996 Act explicitly recognises this in section 2(2)(e) and (m) and section 11(7). Now if you want your neighbour to retain a wall to a greater height than a garden wall, and he originally constructed the wall which he now wants to reduce in height, you must pay your share of the higher portion.

Question 3: what notice do you serve if you're constructing a lift pit adjacent to a party wall? *Short answer:* it all depends. *Longer answer:* it depends on whether you intend to underpin the party wall for your own purposes or not. If you do, then you serve notice under section 3, citing 2(2)(a). If you do not, but the lift pit brings you within either sub-section (1) or (2) of section 6, then you serve notice under sub-section (5) of that section. It could certainly be argued that you do not need to serve twice for one lot of underpinning. However, it cannot be wrong to do so, and if you're a belt and braces man (or the female equivalent), by all means carry on.

Question 4: do you always have to serve notice if your new foundations are lower than those of the next-door building? *Short answer:* yes. *Longer answer:* once again, it's a question of reading the words very carefully. After dealing with the basic three and six metre provisions, the section[1] concludes: 'he (the Building Owner) may, and if required by the adjoining owner shall...underpin or otherwise strengthen or safeguard the foundations of the

---

[1] Section 6(1).

building of the adjoining owner...'. It has been argued from this that you only need to serve notice if you propose to underpin, but just think about it. If you don't serve because you don't intend to underpin, how does the Adjoining Owner know whether to require you to do so? Therefore, dismiss the arguments of those who say that notice is only required if underpinning is proposed: serve.

A supplementary, and very reasonable, question also arises here. What if your foundations are already lower than those of next door, and you propose to rebuild on new foundations no lower, perhaps even slightly less deep than before, but still below your neighbour's? Do you still have to serve notice? The legal answer must be yes.

Question 5: what is 'laying open'?[1] *Answer:* who knows? *More helpful answer:* it doesn't matter as much as it used to. Under the LBA, there was doubt about whether it included simply exposing the party wall to the weather. Most people thought that it did not and that one was not therefore bound to provide protection in those circumstances – although almost everybody did. In the 1996 Act, section 2(2)(n) specifically deals with this point: you may expose the party wall, but you must weather it appropriately.

Question 6: should the named surveyor perform every single function himself? *Some people's answer:* yes. *Authors' answer:* no. Not only does it make the fees prohibitively expensive if the highly qualified expert is going to tramp the streets trying to identify Adjoining Owners, but it also makes him less readily available to deal with the really tricky questions that demand his

---

[1] Section 7(3).

expertise. As is implied in the chapter dealing with fees[1], for juniors' work, use juniors. They are perfectly well able to do a lot of the leg work. They can take schedules and even agree the terms of awards – but must have the authority and supervision of the named surveyor to do so. It is extremely unproductive to send out a representative who has to report back before any decisions are made. The named surveyor, of course, must take full responsibility for those decisions made by his assistant.

Question 7: who is exempt from the Act? *Popular long-held answer:* all those listed in section 151 of the LBA. *Experts' answer:* only those listed in sections 18 and 19 of the 1996 Act. That means the properties of the Inns of Court within Inner London (which were exempt under the LBA) and those properties occupied by the Monarch, the Duchy of Lancaster or the Duchy of Cornwall. Land vested in the Crown, but not occupied in that way, is not exempt, so all government buildings are included.

Question 8: what qualifies for security for expenses? *Frequent answer:* any damage you fear suffering. *Authors' answer:* only the reasonable expectation that you might be left exposed to costs through the default of the Building Owner. For example, if the Building Owner proposes to lay open your premises (really lay open, under section 7(3)), it is perfectly reasonable to require the deposit of a sum which would enable you to replace the wall and enclose yourself again. You should not, though, demand security because a scaffolder might just stick a pole through your window. Section 12 is not, therefore, a general catch-all by which you can demand

---

[1] See Chapter 7.

security because you think the Adjoining Owner's building might suffer damage and the Building Owner might be reluctant or slow to pay.

Question 9: can you raise a party wall on a cantilever? *One answer*: Some people say no. *Authors' answer*: yes. This particular problem arises when you have an old party wall, which has to remain in position while you construct a new building which is going to rise to a greater height. Very often, the best structural answer to the risk of possible damage to the existing wall and its foundations is to carry the new building on its own foundations and frame, and then to construct the new, higher portion of the party wall on a beam sitting over the old wall, cantilevered out from the columns adjacent to the party wall.

In the ordinary meaning of the words, this seems to fall into the definition of 'raising the party wall'. Those in the 'no' camp would argue that as the new structure will be not bearing directly on to the old – there is usually a compression joint between the two – it cannot be said to *stand* on the land of two owners; and it certainly doesn't, being one party's raising separate buildings of two owners. Therefore, they say, it cannot properly be called raising. They are wrong (we think).

Such is the standing of the Pyramus & Thisbe Club that an Official Referee, Judge Esyr Lewis, was once prepared to hear a mock appeal on the subject, in the council chamber of the RICS. Two members set themselves up as Building and Adjoining Owners or Surveyors, and briefed two other members as counsel. A brilliantly and succinctly argued case by the outstanding counsel (a well-known author) in favour of the cantilever persuaded the judge that, in common sense terms, the wall was being raised, and thus satisfied the Act. Proponents of the other view have subsequently, reluctantly, accepted such raising.

A new question, 10, arose when the national Building Regulations superseded the London Building Byelaws. Although it probably should have arisen before, the change brought the problem to the fore. As a one-hour fire resistance is all that is needed to satisfy the law, can an Adjoining Owner insist on a greater period of resistance? Opinion has not yet crystallised on the correct solution, but there seem already to be two answers. If the Building Owner is rebuilding a party wall, he cannot substitute a wall which is in any way less suitable for the Adjoining Owner's purposes than that which it replaces. On the other hand, if he is raising the party wall, for his own purposes, he is probably entitled to build it as flimsily as the law allows.

A further refinement of this question has been raised, but not definitively answered. When two abutting walls are each of insufficient strength to satisfy fire regulations, are they in fact a party wall jointly? The argument is that each is performing the function of 'separating buildings', because the other skin cannot do so alone. This really does seem to be stretching the meaning of the words too far, though. The authors would argue that an owner is perfectly entitled to take down his independent wall, regardless of how skimpy his neighbour's wall is.

16 Some leading cases

Leadbetter v Marylebone Corporation, 1905

Not everyone agrees with the verdict in this case, and it is possible it could be overturned on slightly different facts. However, its continuing relevance makes it a good case to start with.

There are a number of interesting sidelines to *Leadbetter* which bear mention in passing, remembering that it dealt with the *London Building Act* 1894, many of the provisions of which have been substantially re-enacted down to 1996. Indeed, the words of the 1996 Act are not dissimilar. The parties in this case had had an earlier award by which the Corporation was entitled to raise the party wall in the future. When it proceeded to do so, Leadbetter got an injunction because it hadn't served notice. The judge, however, granted the injunction in terms which allowed Marylebone to proceed as soon as it had an award for its new works.

Notice was duly served but, as the parties were at such odds, it took a very long time to agree upon a Third Surveyor and get the awards made. Six months after the service of notice, there was still no award, so the plaintiffs held that the notice was now invalid, and sought execution of the earlier judgment in their favour.

The defendants argued that the six months' validity only applied in cases where the work was consented to, not where there was a difference. The court held that this contention was correct. If proceedings between appointed surveyors delayed matters for more than six months, it was very hard on the Building Owner if he had to start *de novo*.

The words of the relevant section of the 1894 Act were: 'a party wall or structure notice shall not be available for the exercise of any right unless the work to which the notice relates is begun within six months after the service thereof' and the words of section 47(3) were very little different in 1939: 'a party structure notice shall not be effective unless the work to which the notice relates is begun within six months after the notice has been served'. There is not really any substantive difference between the two. The words of the 1996 Act are slightly different, at section 3(2)(b), but not, it seems, in substance, except for doubling the six months to 12. 'A party structure notice shall...cease to have effect if the work to which it relates –

> (i) has not begun within the period of twelve months beginning with the day on which notice is served...'.

Lord Justice Mathew held that this section only applied where no difference arose, and said that he could find no indication in the Act that the limit of six months was to apply when there was a difference. This may strike you (and has certainly struck others) as specious reasoning to justify an equitable decision. Marylebone thought they had the right to build, and started to do so; stopped by Leadbetter until they had obtained an award, they promptly served notice; proceedings thereafter were protracted, doubtless by Leadbetter's side, who then withdrew from negotiations and tried to secure an injunction calling for the pulling down of building to which Marylebone had tried to give legal standing. It was, therefore, equitable to find a loophole for Marylebone. But was it right?

Examine the judgment. 'That sub-section appears to me to provide for cases in which...the adjoining owner consenting thereto, no difference arises...' . Why? Where does the section say anything about consent? The judge went on. 'I cannot see any indication in the Act that the limit of six months...is to apply...to a case where there is a difference'. Of course there isn't, because if it applies generally, there is no need to specify that it applies where there is dissent. The judge's reasoning therefore doesn't seem to hold water. And under the 1996 Act, it could certainly be argued that the 12 months is always definitive.

The advice that can be extrapolated from this case is, if you haven't completed an award 12 months after serving notice, serve new notices.

Selby v Whitbread, 1917

If ever there was a case that proves how impossible it is for a Building Owner to shrug off his responsibilities, this is it. In this important leading case, the surveyors, having reserved to themselves the right to do so in their original award, made an addendum award after the land in question had been dedicated as a highway, so that the Building Owner no longer owned or controlled it: yet the addendum was held to be valid.

There was a pair of buildings in Royal Mint Street about 200 years old, and one of the pair set out to reconstruct itself 13 feet back from its former building line. The result of this was to expose the whole height of the party wall for this distance. The original award concerned with the demolition and reconstruction had said that the Building Owner was to 'take every precaution for the support of the building of the Adjoining Owner...'.

Shortly after the works were completed, the now open land adjoining the party wall was sold to the old London County Council and the land dedicated to the public. Shortly after that, the Adjoining Owner's Surveyor wrote to ask the Building Owner's Surveyor what he proposed to do to support the party wall and the premises behind it. The Building Owners and, you will be sorry to hear, their surveyor, declined to take any further action, claiming that they had offloaded their responsibility on to the LCC. The Third Surveyor was called in by Selby's surveyor, and they made an award calling on Whitbread to put up a substantial pier, and do some other minor works. That award was appealed.

The remarks of McCardie, J. are of great interest. He said that if a Building Owner could discharge his liabilities by selling his property to another, it would seriously diminish the rights of Adjoining Owners, and that transfer to a man of straw would deprive an Adjoining Owner of his proper remedy against the initiator of building operations. He stated that he had read with care the *London Building Act*, and that he found no section to allow a transfer of liability nor one that implied it. 'I should require a clear provision of the statute before holding that such a transmission of liability could take place against the will, and perchance without the knowledge, of the Adjoining Owner.' 'It seems to me,' he added, 'that that section [the one requiring security, now 12] contemplates that the person who serves the notice...shall be and remain liable for all the results which follow from such notice.' The jurisdiction of the surveyors remains in full force until 'the final adjustment of all questions in difference'.

This judgment is in fact studded with words of guidance for party wall surveyors throughout, and it would do you no harm to read it all. It is noteworthy that the judge frequently referred to the surveyors as arbitrators, which must give some support to the arguments advanced elsewhere that that is what they are: certainly not agents for their Appointing Owners. In doing so, he emphasised that 'the primary function of the arbitrators is to safeguard the interests of the Adjoining Owner; although they must, of course, consider the rights and interests of the Building Owner'. In other words, and far too many so-called party wall surveyors forget this, both surveyors have a duty to both Owners, not only to the one that appointed them.

The next gem that warrants selection is the judge's comments on the validity of an award if part of it was invalid. At one time it had been considered that any defect voided the whole award. Later practice held that if the bad could be separated from the good it should be done, and the rest of the award upheld, and McCardie, J. thought that the Court should support an award rather than destroy it, if possible.

The defendants had claimed that some of the works awarded to be done were unnecessary. Even if that was so, the judge thought that the surveyors' decision on that point should be upheld, as it was a matter of expert knowledge, falling most appropriately within the jurisdiction of the arbitrators.

The final extract from this case is also very important, but still open to argument. The judge held that where common law rights and party wall legislation are inconsistent, then the statutory conditions override the common law. McCardie, J. added that a plaintiff could still bring an action if the defendant had exercised his Building Act rights negligently or improperly.

What a case. All party wall surveyors should go on pilgrimage to Royal Mint Street to celebrate.

Bond v Nottingham Corporation, 1940

The main reason for including this case is its bearing on other party wall cases, particularly *Bradburn v Lindsay*.

In this case it was held by Sir Wilfred Greene, later Lord Greene, Master of the Rolls, that an owner was 'under no obligation to repair that part of his building which provided support for his neighbour'. He could therefore eventually allow his neighbour's property to fall down, although he could not, of course, do something positive to withdraw support. However, his neighbour did not have to sit by and watch his support crumble away. He could enter the next-door property and restore support himself.

With the exception of party wall legislation and the *Access to Neighbouring Land Act* 1992, this seems to be the only case that gives a right of entry to a neighbour's premises. In London, of course, you didn't need to take advantage of Bond as, if any decay or damage threatened the party wall itself, you could serve notice under what used to be section 46(1)(a) of the LBA, requiring both parties to contribute to the works of repair. If necessary, you could also enforce entry under what was section 53. The same now applies nationally, under section 2(2)(b) and section 8 of the 1996 Act.

Phipps v Pears, 1964

Although one of the judges in the Court of Appeal said, *obiter*, in the case of *Marchant*[1], that he would be prepared to consider reversing *Phipps v Pears*, it is still good law at the time of writing. This is not strictly speaking a party wall case, but it has a great deal of relevance.

There were two old houses in Warwick. One was pulled down in about 1930, and a new house constructed abutting, but not bonded to, the remaining property. In 1962, the older property was pulled down in its turn, leaving the newer wall exposed. This wall, built against the older, was rather unsuitable for such exposure to the elements, being unrendered and unpointed. Support did not enter into it: the question was whether you could acquire an easement to protection from the wind and rain.

According to *The Times* of 11 March 1964, the Master of the Rolls (Lord Denning) 'said that every man was entitled to pull down his own house if he liked...there was no such easement known to the law as an easement to be protected from the weather'. It follows from this

[1] See below.

that when a party wall is exposed, it has to be dealt with by award whenever a wall needs it. After all, a damp party wall is no good to either owner, even if the effects are felt sooner by the Adjoining Owner.

Protection is called for in the 1996 Act when property is laid open or when a hitherto protected party wall is exposed. As to when that is, see elsewhere[1].

Gyle-Thompson v Walstreet, 1973

Walstreet served notice on Gyle-Thompson that it intended to take down the 40-foot high wall which formed the external wall of Walstreet's building at the end of Gyle-Thompson's garden, and replace it with an eight foot wall topped with a seven foot, six inches slatted fence. It was admitted that the wall stood astride the boundary. The two surveyors failed to agree on the pulling down, but the Building Owner's Surveyor and the Third Surveyor made an award allowing a modified version of the proposals, which had been agreed with other parties whose gardens were similarly bounded. A fortnight after the award had been given to the Building Owner, his workmen started demolishing the wall, only to be stopped by a policeman called in by Gyle-Thompson, who soon obtained an *ex parte* injunction restraining the demolition.

It was held by Brightman, J. that although the 14 days had elapsed for appeal, that was not relevant if the award was fundamentally bad, which this one was. It was not therefore necessary to decide what constituted 'delivery' if, as alleged, the Adjoining Owner had not received his

---

[1] Chapter 15.

copy as soon as the Building Owner. On the substantive issue, he held that there was no right in the *London Building Act* permanently to reduce the height of a party wall, and you could, therefore, only take down a party wall if you proposed to rebuild it to the same height or higher.

Several people have since effectively used this to extort very considerable payments from Building Owners anxious to lower or remove walls, even when the removal benefited the Adjoining Owners as well. Other people considered this to be simply immoral, and it is why the 1996 Act now allows for such lowering, in strictly controlled circumstances.

Some other matters were also dealt with in the hearing of this case. A second notice had been served, only slightly varying the works, and sent to Gyle-Thompson, care of his appointed surveyor. The judge held that this notice had not been properly served, and it would only have been so if the surveyor had been held out as an agent of the owner. Each notice initiates a new set of proceedings, a possible new dispute and, if so, the fresh appointment of a surveyor, and therefore has to go to the owner himself.

The judge referred to the Adjoining Owners as 'owning' half of the wall, which seemed to be why he thought they could keep it up against the Building Owner's wishes. It was this point in particular that John found contentious. He argued that the wall had almost certainly been built, if under the Act, by one owner paying for the whole 40-foot height, or getting at the very most a garden-wall-sized contribution from the Adjoining Owner. A garden wall was all that the Adjoining Owners needed, wanted or paid for. They were now asking for the benefit of a 40-foot high garden wall, for which they had not paid. Under the 1996 Act, they would now be liable to be asked to contribute under section 11(7), for making additional use of a party wall[1], or else bound to let the wall be reduced to garden wall height. John always felt that the same was in fact true under the former legislation, but that this point was not well argued before the court in this case, with the costs of an appeal too great to make the matter of principle worth pursuing.

Bennett v Howell, 1981

Mr Howell's architect had advised him that the wall in question was not a party wall and so, although Mrs Bennett knew what the situation was, no 'formal' notice had been served. At the very last minute, a certain rights of light expert who had been called in was casually asked to confirm that the wall was not party, but gave the contrary opinion. A letter was then put through Mrs Bennett's door informing her that the works would be starting in a couple of days' time and that although she had agreed that it was not a party wall, she was being given notice confirming the earlier information. Mrs Bennett did nothing until the works actually started, when she issued a writ. Eventually, surveyors were formally appointed on both sides and the Adjoining Owner's Surveyor insisted on notice being served on 'the proper forms'. Because time was of the essence, his erroneous wish was complied with, although he was already in possession of a draft award. The Building Owner's Surveyor was unfamiliar with the RIBA (Royal Institute of British Architects) form used and missed out a

---

[1] See Chapter 10.

date on it. He rang the Adjoining Owner's Surveyor and asked him to insert it and was told it would be done. However, the copy eventually produced in Court by Mrs Bennett was not dated!

The two surveyors agreed and signed an award, but Mrs Bennett persisted with her action. The judge held that the award was void because it was dated before the finally dated notices had been served, and that the combination of letters from architects and Building Owners could not be construed as constructive notice. He therefore awarded Mrs Bennett an injunction restraining Mr Howell from carrying out any works until proper notice was served and a new award agreed.

The extraordinary and instructive point to be learnt from this case is that the injunction actually availed Mrs Bennett nothing. Two months later, exactly the same works were carried out, in accordance with an award in exactly the same terms. Her property was not at any serious risk of damage, nor did it suffer any. All that happened was that Mr Howell was put to considerable expense, and had to put up with a building site in his kitchen for another two months. All this, because of a couple of technical flaws in procedure. One might ask whether an injunction was really appropriate in the circumstances. However, one should undoubtedly learn the importance of crossing every 't' and dotting every 'i', as the courts will always require the procedures to be followed precisely (as indeed Brightman, J. had specifically said in *Gyle-Thompson*).

John would have told you that Mrs Bennett disagreed with this report of the case, but she did not manage to convince him that it contained substantial inaccuracies.

Marchant v Capital and Counties, 1983

In 1969, Capital and Counties redeveloped the
Pantechnicon. This was an ancient storage warehouse
with very substantial walls. Many, many years ago,
Mrs Marchant's predecessors had built a mews cottage
against the rear wall of the warehouse, using it as one
wall of their building. That part of the wall against which
they enclosed had become, therefore, a party wall under
section 44(ii) of the LBA, now definition (b) in section
20. Capital and Counties' proposals envisaged leaving the
wall standing as a boundary wall, but with no building
against it on their side. Of course, they had to leave
enough of it up to enclose Mrs Marchant's house.

While the works were being carried out, it was expected
that there might be some exposed pockets of brickwork
from which beams had been removed, and which might
therefore cause some damp problems to Mrs Marchant.
The two surveyors agreed that these would need dealing
with, and stated in their award that the Building Owner
was at liberty to carry out any weatherproofing to the
wall necessary while the works were being done.

Many years later, Mrs Marchant was suffering from
damp in her walls and brought an action against Capital
and Counties. The High Court judge dismissed her action
as being out of time, not covered by common law, and
not arising out of the award. Mrs Marchant's surveyor
had, unfortunately, died, but the judge had the benefit of
hearing evidence from Capital and Counties' surveyor.
Mrs Marchant appealed, and the Court of Appeal, who
of course did not hear evidence, decided that the
surveyors meant to include the weatherproofing in the
part of the award which dealt with what the Building

Owner must do, and that it was meant to be a continuing liability, not just while the works were being carried out. Mrs Marchant's claim was therefore not time-barred!

Courts are entitled to find that documents don't mean what their authors intended them to mean, but many felt that this particular decision was taking that liberty to extremes. The important aspect of the judgments in this case is that surveyors are now held to be capable of imposing continuing liabilities on their owners by award, which was previously thought not to be the case.

Bradburn v Lindsay, 1983

This is a rather difficult case as to how far a neighbour's duty extends. Mrs Lindsay neglected her house, despite complaints from Mr Bradburn as early as 1972. Eventually the house was so derelict that Mrs Lindsay allowed the council to pull it down in 1977. From the earlier neglect and later exposure, the Bradburns' house became thoroughly dry-rotted, as well as exposed to weather and suffering some subsidence cracks.

The case was carefully distinguished from *Phipps v Pears*[1] because the two properties in it shared a common wall or, in the case of the roof void, a lack of it. *Bond v Nottingham Corporation*[2], which postulated a right to self-help, was also brought in, but Judge Blackett-Ord held that the right to take measures for your own benefit did not relieve another party of any duty which he might owe you (citing *Leakey v National Trust*, 1980). Accordingly, the Bradburns were awarded damages for

[1] See above.
[2] See above.

the dry rot, plus reasonable works to make the 'party walls' secure against further inroads.

Brace v SE Regional Housing Association Ltd, 1984

The critical element of this case for party wall surveyors is only a small part of a much larger whole. The matter concerned a 'party wall' in Harrow, outside the *London Building Act*, but the two surveyors dealt with it more or less in accordance with 'inside the Act' procedures, by a party structure agreement.

After the property that belonged to the Building Owner (the Housing Association) was pulled down, Mrs Brace noticed cracking and subsidence. One of the defendant's answers to the subsequent claim was that Mrs Brace's surveyor had agreed an 'award', and that as that award had been complied with, Mrs Brace had no further right of support.

The Court of Appeal held that entering into an agreement (and that rule might well apply to an award) was not to be construed as a giving up of any rights of support. If one party wished to rely upon abandonment, they would have to prove the existence of that intention in express terms, and no such terms were to be found.

It is of interest that the operative clause was in somewhat vague terms: 'The Building Owner shall be at liberty...to strengthen, repair or underpin' the party wall. It was therefore clearly left to the Housing Association to decide whether and how to support the wall. It might be argued that if a specific form of works had been agreed by her surveyor and accepted by the Adjoining Owner, there would have been more chance of substantiating an allegation that Mrs Brace had surrendered her rights.

In an unreported case inside the Act, with which John was peripherally involved, it was alleged that the Adjoining Owner's Surveyor (if that's what he was in law – see the next point) was liable, along with the Building Owner and his surveyor, for the collapse of the Adjoining Owner's building. In this particular case, almost every procedural action was carried out incorrectly, thus complicating an already tricky situation. The two surveyors had perhaps never been properly appointed, and their award may well thus have been void *ab initio* and its strictures unenforceable. In the end though, it was held (or conceded – John couldn't quite remember), that the prime responsibility remained with the Building Owner.

One further sideline on this latter case. John once suggested that if the Adjoining Owner's Surveyor had been appointed under the Act, he couldn't be sued for negligence, as an arbitrator; if he hadn't been properly appointed, he had no such immunity. As far as Graham is aware, this basic contention has not been settled, but he thinks you would have difficulty suing a party wall surveyor.

To conclude: an Adjoining Owner's rights are not lightly given away, and responsibility rests with the Building Owner unless there is strict proof to the contrary.

Lehmann v Herman, 1992

This case proves the importance of serving correct notices. Mr Herman served notice on his neighbour of his intention to do some works which would have had a minimal – if any – effect on Mr Lehmann's land and property. The latter objected that Mr and Mrs Herman were joint owners of the property, and should both have

served notice. Mr Herman refused to re-serve and
Mr Lehmann sued. The court found that the couple were
'in *the* occupation' (our italics) of the property, under the
LBA, and so should both have signed. New wording in
the 1996 Act avoids this, but the case emphasises the
need for precision in notices.

Woodhouse v Consolidated Property, 1992

Before this case, many surveyors ignored the precise date
of service of notice, and settled any matters in dispute
regardless of the date of their cause or occurrence. Under
the LBA, their powers to arbitrate arose from the notice,
and so when an eminent expert made a Third Surveyor's
award concerning damage which had occurred before
notice had been served, and his award was later brought
into question in other court proceedings, he was ruled to
be acting *ultra vires*.

The 1996 Act gives the surveyors power to deal with
matters arising out of the Act – a much wider scope – so
the question should not arise in this form again.
However, a lesson remains: you must only deal in an
award with those matters which are within your remit as
a party wall surveyor.

Louis v Sadiq, 1996

The most interesting point in this case had nothing to do
with party walls as such, but arose out of a failure to
proceed properly. John was the Third Surveyor here, but
not involved in the subsequent legal proceedings.

Mr Sadiq took down the entire front wall of his house
(and various other bits) without any notice to Mrs Louis,

whose house soon began to suffer in consequence. The Third Surveyor was called in – more than once – and made various awards as to how the fabric was to be reinstated.

Subsequently, Mrs Louis brought proceedings against Mr Sadiq for the losses she had suffered as a result of his unauthorised and unnotified activities. Among those losses were the additional costs of building a house in Guadaloupe (which she had planned to do with the proceeds of the sale of the London house), which had risen considerably since she had embarked on the proposal. The court held that this was a direct consequence of Mr Sadiq's wrongful actions, and he should therefore pay.

As with *Brace* (above), a Building Owner was found to be liable for the results of his actions. In the Sadiq case, these might well have been avoided if he had served notice, and surveyors been appointed who would have taken steps to protect Mrs Louis's property.

The Great Wall of Knightsbridge, 1998

The real title of this case is *Prudential v Waterloo*, but it was given its nickname by one of the solicitors, and many prefer it!

You may acquire the further face of a party wall by adverse possession. Some may find this bald statement hard to accept, but in the paragraphs that follow, we will explain the judge's reasoning.

A great deal of this case, which lasted 32 days in court, was taken up with the history of the wall from the very beginning of the 18th century. After following the wall through all the changes on both sides of it, the judge came to the conclusion that it had been a party wall, and that both Prudential and Waterloo had paper title to their respective portions.

He then dealt with the adverse possession claim advanced by Waterloo. The building which used to stand on the Prudential's side had been demolished, and the alignment of the street altered, so that the wall was now adjoining the pavement. Waterloo had made openings in the wall, rendered it, decorated it, and raised it to carry a roof over a former yard on their land, all without seeking consent from or demur by the Prudential. Accordingly, said the judge, the Pru had given up or been ousted from possession of their half of the wall (there was no argument about it having been for the requisite 12 years) and Waterloo had acquired it.

The particular circumstances of this case are not likely to recur, but you should be warned that walls can – just – change from party to sole ownership. Millions of pounds hung on this case, but even garden walls have their price.

Loost v Kremer, 1997

This case, an appeal to the Third Surveyor's award under the LBA, has a number of points which are of equal interest and relevance to the 1996 Act.

Mr Loost and Mr Kremer lived in adjoining houses in a terrace. Mr Loost owned the freehold of his, while Mr Kremer was the leaseholder of the second and third floors of his. His freeholder, Mrs Bartholomew, lived in the lower maisonette. Mr Kremer intended to enlarge the top floor, by inserting beams into the party wall, raising the parapet wall and changing the slope of his roof. These works needed a licence from Mrs Bartholomew, which was duly given.

The first point of party wall interest concerns that old chestnut: does a leaseholder whose demise is limited to the plaster own a sufficient interest in the wall to make him an owner? In 1995, that was Mr Kremer's position, but in January 1996, to deal with that specific point (and answer the question: no) his lease was varied to give him an interest in his 'half' of the party wall. A relevant matter is that His Honour Judge Cowell was of the opinion that Mr Kremer's leasehold interest extended up to the top of the parapets.

Mr Loost objected to an award by the Third Surveyor on several grounds. He said that Mrs Bartholomew should have joined in the notice, as freeholder, and it was therefore invalid; the Deed of Variation was an artifice insufficient to make Mr Kremer an owner; some drawings were unclear; and the appointment of Mr Kremer's surveyor (also the architect for the scheme) was improper. The Third Surveyor (someone who may be familiar to you by now, and it wasn't John) was called in to decide the validity of the notice and the alleged conflict of interest caused by Mr Kremer's party wall surveyor also being the architect. He decided that the notice was in order and so was the appointment of the surveyor.

The judge examined the definitions of 'owner' and 'building owner' in the 1930 *London Building Act*, carried over into the 1939 Act, as well as the definitions of a party wall. He concluded that Mr Loost and Mr Kremer were both owners under the Act, so the only question remaining was whether Mrs Bartholomew was the Building Owner.

As it was Mr Kremer who wanted to carry out the work as a leaseholder of the building, he was a 'building owner' and 'desirous of building'. Mrs Bartholomew did not need to be named in the notice.

However, the really interesting part is that Mr Loost pleaded that the Third Surveyor did not have the jurisdiction to decide the two matters settled in his award: that Mr Kremer's architect could also be his surveyor and that Mrs Bartholomew did not have to join in the notice.

According to Judge Cowell, these two points were absolutely fundamental and an 'arbitrator, a third surveyor, does have the jurisdiction to decide a matter, even if it is a matter of law, which is fundamental to the question of whether he makes an award or not'. While it was open for an arbitrator to say: 'This is a matter of law: let the courts decide it and then come back to me', the judge could see nothing wrong in the arbitrator or Third Surveyor deciding the point, making an award, and leaving it to any aggrieved party to appeal on the point of law.

In the opinion of the authors, this means that in future if the status of a wall, or even its ownership, is questioned, the Third Surveyor can decide this matter and make any other necessary award, leaving it to the parties to appeal if they are not convinced by his decision.

The judge held that not only was the Third Surveyor right in deciding that he was entitled to make the award, but even if he was wrong to do so in law, he, the judge, would make a declaration that the decisions the Third Surveyor reached in that award were correct. He had even been correct in producing his award when Mr Loost's surveyor had gone on holiday, as the judge could not see anything further which could properly have been put before him.

Arena Property Services Ltd v Europa 2000 Ltd, 2003

In this case Arena served notice on an Adjoining Owner (in effect, Europa's predecessor) to remove a boiler flue and soil vent pipe which ran over the top of the party wall from the adjoining property at first floor level, then down Arena's side near to ground level and back through the party wall to the adjoining building. The soil vent pipe served the upper floors of the adjoining property.

Arena served notice on the freeholders of the adjoining property, Mr Macit and Mr Bas on 17 November 2000. Unbeknown to Arena (and presumably the surveyors), Messrs Macit and Bas subsequently granted a 99-year lease to Europa of those upper floors served by the soil pipe.

The surveyors made an award on 8 October 2001 providing for these projections to be removed. The award was between Arena and Messrs Macit and Bas. In March of the following year, the soil pipe was removed from Arena's side of the party wall. Meanwhile, Europa refurbished their floors. However, from August 2002 they were unable to let those floors because of the absence of a soil pipe.

The appeal to the surveyors' award arose from Europa's counterclaim for compensation for loss and damage as an Adjoining Owner under section 7(2) of the 1996 Act.

162

The County Court judge held that the surveyors' award could extinguish the easement (although an easement had not been established) and that Europa were not entitled to compensation because they were not being deprived by Arena of any right they had. Section 7(2) could not be so widely construed as to give compensation for the 'inevitable permanent and lawful consequences of implementing the Award'.

Europa appealed. The Court of Appeal held that as Europa's interest in the property had been carved out of the freehold interest after the original notice had been served, they were the successor in title to the Adjoining Owner on whom the notice was served.

Europa's interest was at first floor level and above. The offending soil pipe was at ground level, yet the Court decided that Europa were an Adjoining Owner, even though the works did not affect the area of party wall upon which Europa were enclosed. Nonetheless, the Appeal Court stated that the County Court judge was correct to conclude that no easement had been established and that Arena had the right to remove the projection.

Roadrunner Properties Ltd v Dean & Suffolk & Essex, 2004

Dean carried out works to their property, which included chasing a channel into the party wall for central heating pipes. The contractor used a Kango hammer drill to form the chase. The Adjoining Owner claimed that damage had been caused to the party wall and the adjacent floor tiles.

Dean had not served notice on the Adjoining Owner, even though it was clear the wall was party and they intended to cut into it. As a consequence, there was no schedule of condition of the adjoining building.

The Building Owner's defence was that it was a coincidence that damage arose in the adjoining building after the Kango had attacked the wall, because the floor tiles had been affected by climatic change. Unfortunately, Dean failed to provide any evidence to support this view.

The Court of Appeal said that as there was no evidence that the defects had been caused by something other than the works to the party wall, Dean should be liable. Sedley, LJ said that these works and the vibration caused by them were the most likely cause of the damage. Importantly, the judge said: 'if there was a want of direct evidence, it was the fault of the First Defendant (Dean) in not giving a Party Wall Notice'.

The moral of the story is to ensure that notices are served. If you think the works are minor, then take a schedule of condition of the adjoining property.

Graham is often asked whether the removal of plaster from a party wall requires notice. Before this case, he would have said no, but would have noted that a schedule of condition should be taken. Following this case, he would now advise you to serve notice and have schedules prepared even for such a minor work.

* * *

And that is just about all the authors can think of to tell you about party walls, apart from the Appendices which follow (some of which are of even more marginal relevance than the asides in the main body of this work). That doesn't mean there isn't anything else to say, though. Graham would agree with John's view that almost every day brings some new little twist to an expert's attention; it is salutary to realise that in just 15 pages of legislation (for the 1996 Act), there can be so many subtleties. Each previous edition of this book has attempted to incorporate all changes and variations, and this new edition has tried to do the same.

To conclude, the authors would leave you with this admonition. Keep the Act to hand, and never be afraid or ashamed to say to a questioner: 'Just a moment while I see exactly what the Act says'. John was always sure to take his own advice in that respect (while writing this book and in other areas), and passed on this good practice to Graham. It is the authors' fervent hope that it has paid off.

Appendix I

Un peu d'histoire

(as Michelin puts it)

When the first edition of this book was written, the earliest reference John could find to party walls was in the Ten Books on Architecture by Vitruvius, written around the year dot, ±50. Not everything he has to say is of immediate relevance in the world of high-tech building, but he did make reference to party walls. In Book II, Chapter VIII he offered advice on this subject, which conflicts, unfortunately, with section 11[1] of the 1996 Act: 'When arbitrators are appointed to value party walls, they do not value them at what they cost to build, but they look at the original contract and then deduct one-eightieth of the cost for every year that the wall has been built in order to arrive at its present-day value.'

Later, the archaeologist Tim Tatton-Brown told John of the Pergamum Building By-Laws, enacted in about 200 BC. After dealing with highways (width and maintenance of) and refuse (disposal of) they get down to party walls. Where repairs are needed and one party is reluctant, he has to pay three-fifths, instead of half, the cost. There is also very useful guidance on a problem we have today still not solved definitively: where both parties use a wall equally, they pay equally for its repair, but where a wall has a building on one side and an open area

---

[1] See Chapter 10.

on the other, then the costs are defrayed in the proportion of two to one. The same rule is applied to two-storey buildings abutting single-storey ones.

It appears that notice had to be given of any works proposed to party walls, and agreement obtained, and the equivalent of a three-metre notice was also needed if you wanted to dig a trench alongside the party wall. There were very complicated rules about drainage channels when two properties abutted on a slope, but if you want to read about those you'll have to find a copy of *The Greeks in Ionia and the East* by J. M. Cook (Thames and Hudson, 1962). You'll also find a whole article on Roman legislation in *Structural Survey*, Vol. 13 No. 4 (1995), reviewing, among other books, *Ancient Rome: City Planning and Administration* by O. F. Robinson (Routledge, 1992).

Tim, the former director of the Canterbury Archaeological Trust, also told John about a charter of 868 AD, which laid down that, in mid-ninth century Canterbury, there had to be a two-foot gap between houses to allow for eaves drip. This is the earliest written evidence for dense occupation in any town in England.

After this, the list of antiquarian references passes through a dark age until the 14th century: *The London Assize of Nuisance 1301–1431*, a book edited by Dr Helena Chew and William Kellaway (London Record Society, 1973), gives details of party wall cases heard at that time. On Friday, 22 January 1305, it was held that the 'custom of the City does not permit anyone, even though having a share in a stone wall, to demolish his part of it without the consent of his coparcener'. Just like *Gyle-Thompson v Walstreet*! However, in May 1324, it was held that the Building Owner could use a bearing in the wall to the depth of his ownership, and no more.

Many of the disputes arose out of the *Lex de Assisa*, which originated around 1200 and laid down, for example, rather like section 1, that for stone walls three feet thick, each party was to give 18 inches of his land and half the cost. If one party could not or would not build jointly, he had to give all the three feet of land necessary, while the other party built and paid for the wall, and its ownership was then shared.

In 1333, a suit was brought for the rebuilding of a party wall between two privies. The plaintiffs said that 'the extremities of those sitting upon the seats can be seen, a thing which is abominable'. It was ordered, after a site inspection(!), that the wall should be replaced.

Keith McDonald, an eminent and senior party wall surveyor, found a reference to a party wall dispute in Dartmouth, with an award dated 1 March 1429. This held that the Building Owner should take down the pynon wall (a gable) to floor level, and rebuild it of sufficient strength for his purposes at his own expense, supporting the Adjoining Owner's premises the while. Thereafter the wall was to be maintained jointly.

It is not surprising that the Great Fire of London, with its rapid spread, should have led to an Act to control various aspects of building in the City. The Act of 1667 also dealt with a few party wall matters, including agreement between surveyors that party wall foundations had been correctly laid out, and the provision for payment of a half share of the costs by the Adjoining Owner – plus six per cent per annum.

In 1724 an Act was passed which extended control to the cities of both London and Westminster, and to four contiguous parishes. This introduced the idea of the Building Owner giving notice, workmen from both sides arriving at a kind of award, and then work proceeding. The 1764 Act prohibited cutting into party walls for chimneys – very much an anti-fire provision – and this was followed by another Act in the following year which first allowed forcible entry into an Adjoining Owner's premises, armed with an authority from a Justice of the Peace, in order to prevent wilful obstruction (by a difficult neighbour) of reasonable works to a party wall.

The Third Surveyor, except that he is a fifth, appeared in 1772. Two surveyors or able workmen were to be appointed by each side, and a JP had the power to appoint an additional one to help the two sides/four men come to an agreement.

The world of the party wall was substantially enlarged in 1844, when the Building Act concerned itself with 'The Metropolis', an area slightly larger than the County of London. This Act dealt at length with party walls, and virtually all its provisions, together with those of succeeding Acts, were incorporated in the 1894 Act, which we tend to look upon as the real ancestor of our present Acts as, although worded differently, its principles constitute most of what we know today.

A major recasting of the Act took place in 1930, amending legislation was passed in 1935, and in 1939 there came that paragon of Acts, The *London Building Acts (Amendment) Act*. Although Greater London was formed in 1965, the control of the Act was not extended beyond the former County of London where the writ of

1939 ran; but, fortunately, the abolition of Greater London in 1986 contrariwise did not reduce its sway. Many of the provisions of the 1939 Act did disappear with the advent of the Greater London Council (GLC), including the District Surveyor service (much lamented by John – and others), but Part VI rolled on.

Finally (for the time being), the rest of England and Wales woke up to what it was missing – with a little prompting from public-spirited chaps such as John – and the 1996 Act was passed, based very largely on the LBA. Most of the differences have been pointed out during the earlier part of this book. Differences aside, it can still be said that the spirit of the *London Building Acts* lives on in the new legislation, to the great benefit of Building Owners, Adjoining Owners and party wall surveyors.

Appendix II

Who does what

It might be helpful to have a table of who is required to, or has the right to, do what, as it varies between owner and surveyor. Of course, the surveyor can do things on behalf of the owner as his agent, but he must be expressly authorised to do so.

Section	Action	Doer
1(2)	Serve notice	Building Owner
1(3)	Consent	Adjoining Owner
1(5)	Serve notice	Building Owner
3(1)	Serve notice	Building Owner
3(3)(a)	Consent	Adjoining Owner
(1)	Counter-notice	Adjoining Owner
5	Consent	Adjoining Owner
6(5)	Serve notice	Building Owner
6(7)	Consent	Adjoining Owner
6(9)	Supply particulars	Building Owner
8(1)	Enter premises	Building Owner, his servants, agents and workmen
8(2)	Enter closed premises	As 8(1), plus a policeman
8(3)	Notice of entry	Building Owner

Section	Action	Doer
8(5)	Entry	Surveyor
10(1)(a)	Concur in appointment	Both owners
10(1)(b)	Appoint surveyor	Each owner
10(3)	Agreed Surveyor fails	Start again
10(4)	Either owner fails to appoint	The other owner
10(5)	Exit of a surveyor	Original Appointing Owner
10(6)	Surveyor refuses to act	Other surveyor *ex parte*
10(7)	Surveyor fails to act	Other surveyor *ex parte*
10(8)	Surveyor fails or refuses to agree a Third Surveyor	Either surveyor
10(9)	Third Surveyor fails	The other two surveyors
10(10)	Award	Two surveyors or, rarely, one or three
10(11)	Disputed award	Third Surveyor, at the request of either party or either surveyor
10(13)	Costs of award	Surveyors decide, parties pay
10(17)	Appeal	Either owner
11	Expenses	Either owner, or as settled in the award
12	Security for expenses	The owners
13	Account for expenses	The owners

It is worth noting that very little falls to the surveyors: their only function under the Act is to draw up the award. As noted in the rest of the book, however, the surveyor very often does a great deal more, acting as the agent for his Appointing Owner and outside his arbitratory function. In such cases, he must be absolutely certain that he has the requisite authority to do so. If he can wrap it all up in his letter of appointment, so much the better.

Appendix III

Section 10 timetable

Much of this already appears elsewhere, but it may help to have it tabulated.

Action	Time
Either party to appoint a surveyor after written request	10 days
An Agreed Surveyor to act after written request	10 days
Either surveyor to act after written request by either party or the other surveyor	10 days
Third Surveyor to act after written request	10 days
Either party to appeal	14 days

Appendix IV

Idle jottings

Schedules of condition

This, by the way, is a shibboleth. Educated party wall surveyors speak of schedules (plural) of condition (singular). Less well-brought-up chaps speak of conditions (plural). A property may have many rooms, but only one condition.

What is the purpose of an S of C? It is to record the state of those parts of an adjoining building which might be affected by the Building Owner's works. Do not record that the wallpaper is sky-blue pink: even the worst contractor is not likely to sneak in and paint it green overnight. Do say whether it is damp-stained or torn by plaster cracking below it: that is the sort of thing the Adjoining Owner never notices until work starts next door. He then swears – and believes – that the damage was caused by the works.

Note the extent of any existing cracks, and whether they appear to be superficial or to penetrate the fabric of the structure. If necessary, put tell-tales or pencil marks on them. Buy a crack gauge from the Pyramus & Thisbe Club. Count the broken window panes.

It is difficult to know how far to take your schedule. Certainly you must cover the party wall itself and then probably extend into the room, via ceiling, floor and flank walls, up to the first natural break – a window, door, or where there is a change of surface. Such is the nature of the beast, that sometimes you won't have anticipated where the damage will break out. In King's Cross Road there were, for nearly 20 years, signs of damage to the next building but one from a development with which John was once concerned, because the immediately adjacent building was so solid that when it moved – which it did quite enthusiastically – it moved as a whole. No one, of course, had thought of taking a schedule of the building next door to that one, and nor should you. When that sort of thing happens, you just have to use your surveyor's common sense to sort the damage out and attribute blame appropriately.

Don't rely on photographs (new-fangled techniques and equipment notwithstanding), and video is probably even less help. Unless very skilfully taken – and not always then – photographs won't show up the faint cracks that need to be recorded. Use them as an *aide-mémoire* by all means, perhaps overdrawing to indicate the position of a crack. However, sketches are probably just as good, if not better.

Presentation of the schedule is a matter of taste. One possible method is illustrated in the RICS *Party Wall Legislation and Procedure* guidance note. Choose your own style by all means, but always remember that its purpose is to make it easy to recall the original condition of the premises, to be able readily to identify any changes, and to apportion liability.

Agent, arbitrator, or agitator

During the course of a party wall affair, the surveyor may be any or all of these characters. In serving notices, the Building Owner's Surveyor will probably be the first. In trying to get damage put right, the Adjoining Owner's Surveyor may well have to be the last.

The important thing to remember is that most of the time, both surveyors must take on the middle role. The judge in *Selby v Whitbread* referred to the pair of them as arbitrators, and so they are: both conscious of both owners' rights and duties, and not acting – when they have their party wall hats on – as agents for the party who appointed them.

You will have noticed how frequently we use the term 'Appointing Owner' in this book, and how infrequently the word 'client' appears. It is more easy to preserve the correct detachment if you always refer to your Appointing Owner, and avoid calling him your client. Indeed, if you can be said to have a client at all, it is the Act itself.

Appendix V

The Pyramus & Thisbe Club

What on earth, you may ask, does the 'Pyramus & Thisbe Club' have to do with surveying? Most of its members don't understand its title either, and refer to it as the 'P and T'. The relevance, however, is that Pyramus and Thisbe had to converse through a chink in a wall which separated the lands of their respective fathers, in Greek (or Roman) myth. In Shakespeare's version of the lamentable comedy, performed by the rude mechanicals to honour the wedding of Theseus and Hippolyta in *A Midsummer Night's Dream*, Bottom tells Theseus that 'the wall is down that parted their fathers'. This is the motto of the Club which, as you have probably worked out, is concerned with party wall matters.

The Club was founded soon after the case of *Gyle-Thompson v Walstreet*, when many imperfect reports of the judgment in that case were circulating, and it was suggested to John by two members of his staff that there ought to be some forum in which interesting cases could be discussed and points of difference thrashed out. John immediately acted on this suggestion and wrote to every surveyor with whom he had had party wall dealings, inviting them to a get-together to discuss the formation of a club. The response was enthusiastic, and unanimous agreement was reached on nearly every point except the title. A steering committee was elected, with John as the inaugural chairman, told to set up the club on the lines discussed, and to find a generally acceptable name. John was recounting all this to an English teacher friend of his, Paula Morris, who suggested Pyramus and Thisbe. This so delighted John by its aptness that he positively insisted on its adoption by a confused and largely uncomprehending membership.

A couple of years later, the committee decided that the members ought to know under whose colours they were parading, and so a cast containing the then Master of the Worshipful Company of Chartered Surveyors, a past president of the Building Surveyors' Division of RICS, the founder chairman and others presented a substantial chunk of Act V of *A Midsummer Night's Dream* to a wondering audience. To celebrate the passing of the 1996 Act, a further production was mounted with a different cast.

The Club is, on the whole, a serious working body for the improvement of knowledge and understanding of party walls and associated subjects, and has attracted a host of distinguished speakers from the surveying, construction and legal professions. There have been debates on contentious points, brains trusts, lectures from members, and practical demonstrations. The Club has mounted seminars on party walls and contributed the bulk of the working party which produced the RICS guidance note, *Party Wall Legislation and Procedure*. A biannual conference is also held (with the most recent one attended by over 250 people). The Club's website, providing even more information, can be accessed at www.partywalls.org.uk.

The only qualification for membership is an active interest in party walls – no profession is excluded, and no exam has to be passed. Some architects and some engineers and lawyers belong, as do several former District Surveyors, and every grade of building surveyor from trainee to senior members of RICS (including past presidents of the Building Surveyors' Division).

The Christmas lunch of the Club is usually well attended, by the President of RICS, the Faculty President, the Chairman of the District Surveyors' Association and other luminaries, including occasionally the more enlightened Presidents of the Royal Institute of British Architects (RIBA). Entertainment has been provided annually, although members are now sadly deprived of the parodies written and sung by John. Graham so far shows no signs of picking up John's mantle in this respect.

In 1989 the Club set up a working party to report on various vexed questions of interpretation of the LBA, and to make suggestions as to possible improvements. The group produced a complete report, and took counsel's opinions on some knotty legal points. The results were published in a green-covered booklet and then debated by the entire membership. Their views were all recorded and a definitive book for general sale was duly produced, also with a green cover and hence known as 'The Green Book'. The second edition of that work deals with the new Act (its full name is *The Party Wall Act Explained*, and is available from RICS Books), and a third edition is nearing publication. It was, of course, another working party from the Club which drafted the 1996 Act itself.

Since the coming into force of the new Act, the P&T has greatly expanded, and branch clubs have sprung up all over the country, with over 850 members. A national register has been published of members of all the branches, which has been sent to all local authorities and Citizens Advice Bureaux, and is regularly revised and brought up to date.

The authors hope that some of the above is of interest, and in any case, should give you a fairly full idea of the Club's nature. The important thing to note is that it really is a fount of party wall wisdom and opinion (though not always the same opinion). Anyone with an obscure problem should be sure of assistance by contacting the Club, through RICS if necessary. There will always be someone prepared to advise a fellow professional in distress.

Very select bibliography

Readers should note that all of these publications may be ordered from RICS Books, via the website www.ricsbooks.com.

Anstey, J., *Access To Neighbouring Land Act, 1992*, College of Estate Management, Reading, 1993

Anstey, J. and Powell, D., *Anstey's Boundary Disputes and How To Resolve Them* (3rd edition), RICS Books, Coventry, 2004

Anstey, J. and Vegoda, V., *An Introduction to the Party Wall etc. Act 1996*, Lark Productions, London, 1997

Bickford-Smith, S. and Sydenham, C., *Party Walls: Law and Practice* (2nd edition), Jordan Publishing Ltd, Bristol, 2004

Chynoweth, P., *The Party Wall Casebook*, Blackwell Publishing, Oxford, 2003

Hannaford, S. and Stephens, J., *Party Walls – Case in Point*, RICS Books, Coventry, 2004

Pyramus & Thisbe Club, *The Party Wall Act Explained (the 'Green Book')* (2nd edition), London, 1997

RICS, *Party Wall Legislation and Procedure* (5th edition), RICS guidance note, RICS Books, Coventry, 2002

RICS, *Party Wall Legislation and Procedure – Notices and Letters CD-ROM*, RICS Books and Andrew Dyke Associates Ltd, Coventry, 2002

RICS Books, *The Party Wall etc. Act 1996 – Best Practice 2002*, RICSoundtrack (previously Owlion Audio Programme), Coventry, 2002

Useful websites

Pyramus & Thisbe Club: www.partywalls.org.uk

Party Wall Discussion Forum: ww.partywallforum.co.uk

RICS party wall information: www.rics.org/property/management/easements

Index

Note: Bold figures indicate principal entries

abandonment of rights 155–6
access, right of **101–6**, 171
  broad scope of Section 8
    104–6
  for non-Act reasons 101–2
  notice for 72
  possible for Section 1 works 42
  refusal to allow 130
  for repair or support 147–8
  for Third Surveyor 97
  to be covered in award 60, 81
*Access to Neighbouring Land
  Act* (Anstey) 101, 147
  John Anstey's book on 101
accounts 118
Act vii-viii, 157
  area of operation 42
  buildings erected prior to Act
    36
  essential *vade mecum* for
    surveyors viii, 165
  Section 1 41–2
  Section 2 22, 27, **31–6**, 44,
    109, 111, 112, 137, 138
  Section 3 63, 71, 72
  Section 4 71, 72
  Section 5 (implied) 72
  Section 6 37–41, 63
  Section 7 162–3
  Section 8 102–6, 148
  Section 9 132–3
  Section 10 71, 106, 117, 128,
    174

Section 11 59, 112–15, 124,
  130
Section 12 115–18, 139–40
Section 13 118
Section 14 118
Section 15 67
Section 16 130
Section 17 130
Section 18 139
Section 19 139
Section 20 153
Acts, earlier
  1724 169
  1772 169
  1844 169
  1894 142–4, 145, 169
  1930 160–1, 169
  1935 169
  1939 *see London Building Acts
    (Amendment) Act* (LBA)
addendum award 52, 61, 144
adjoining: defined 1
Adjoining Owner
  change of identity during work
    121–4
  change of ownership 119–24
  consent to special foundations
    71, 72
  counter-notices 71–2
  dissent to changes after consent
    54
  duty to appoint surveyor 6–8